LONDON'S NORTH BANK IN 50 BUILDINGS

LOUIS BERK & RACHEL KOLSKY

AMBERLEY

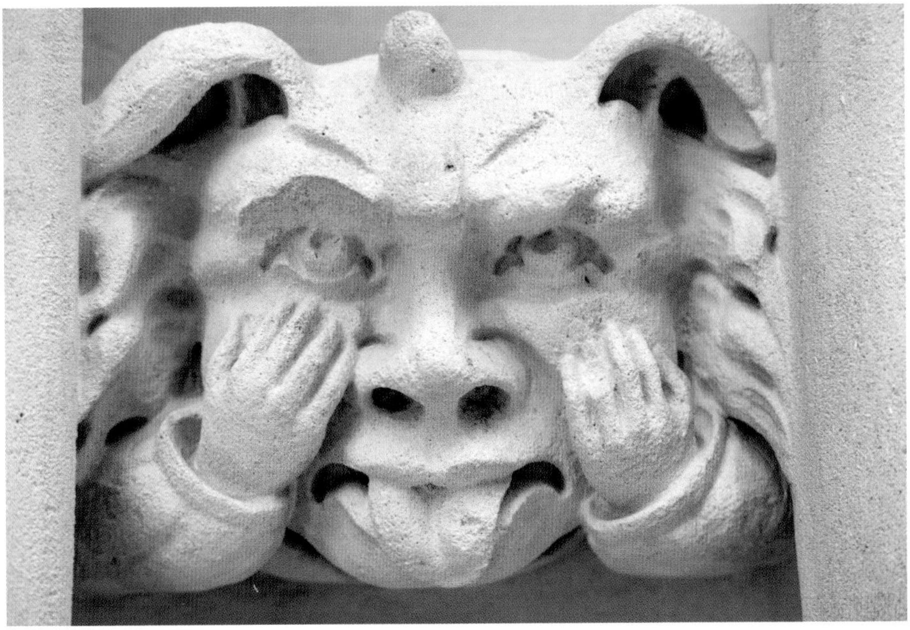

Playful gargoyle at Sion Hall.

First published 2024

Amberley Publishing, The Hill, Stroud
Gloucestershire GL5 4EP

www.amberley-books.com

British Library Cataloguing in Publication Data.
A catalogue record for this book is available from the British Library.

ISBN 978 1 3981 1029 8 (print)
ISBN 978 1 3981 1030 4 (ebook)

Typesetting by SJmagic DESIGN SERVICES, India.
Printed in Great Britain.

Contents

How to use this book

The buildings are listed as seen walking eastwards from the north end of Vauxhall Bridge towards Tower Bridge. Where an entry is a listed building, this indicates it is designated a nationally important and protected building, graded by Historic England (historicengland.org.uk). The map, indicative only and not to scale, enables you to locate the buildings within the book, as the key uses the same numbers as the text. Information regarding transport and websites was correct at the time of writing. Transport for London (tfl.gov.uk) is an excellent resource for planning journeys, and before visiting any of the buildings with public access it is advisable to check their individual websites for opening hours. Each entry has the full address and postcode for ease of locating.

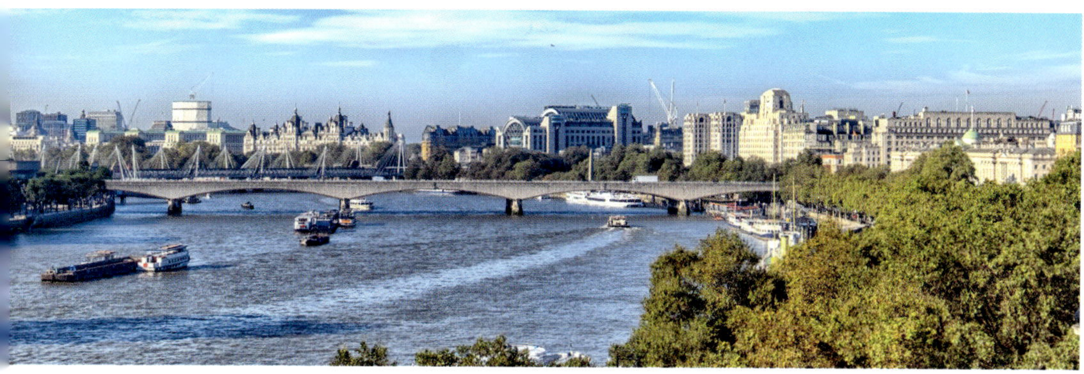

The North Bank looking west from Carmelite House.

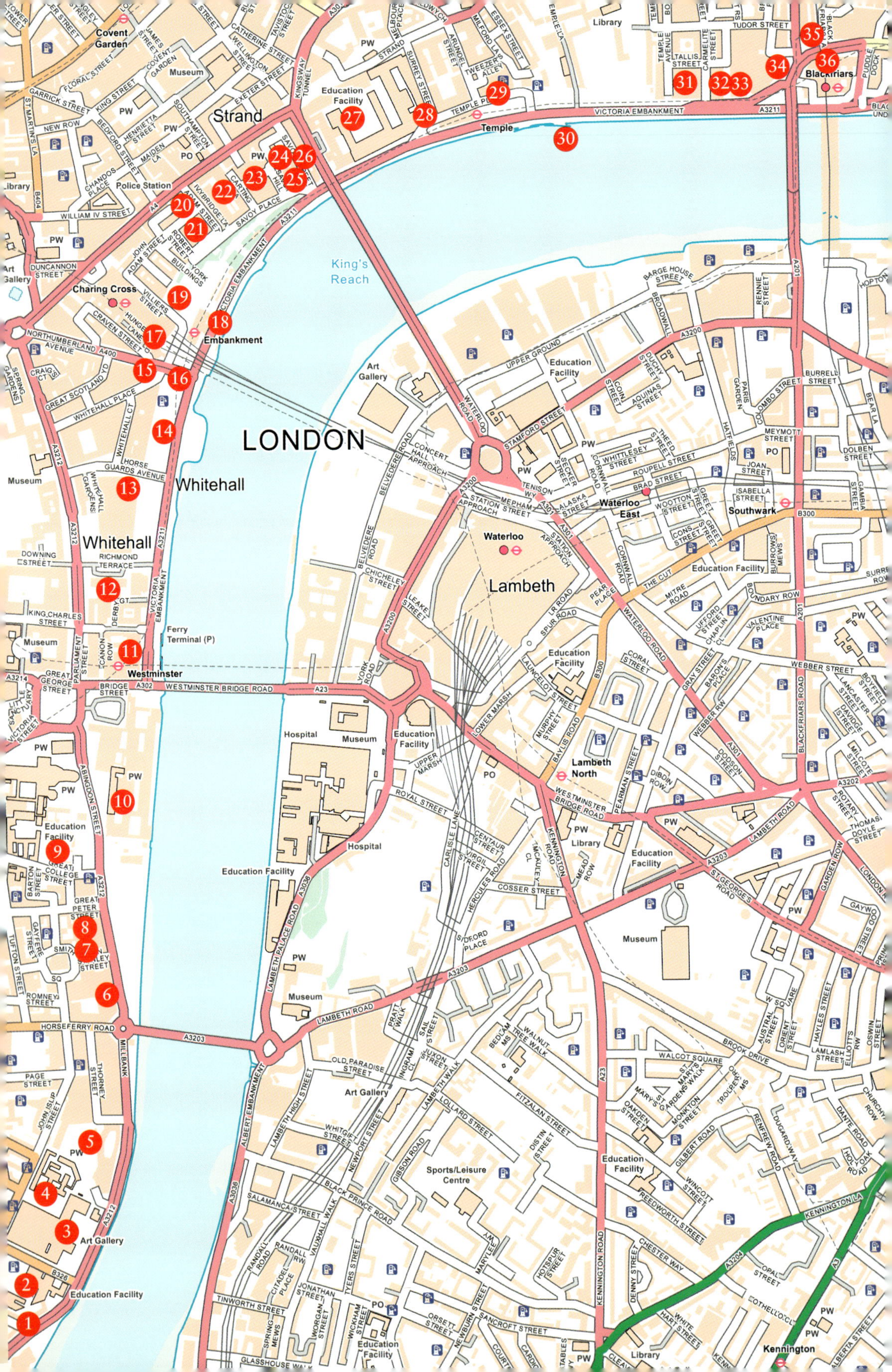

LONDON
Covent Garden
Strand
Charing Cross
Embankment
King's Reach
Whitehall
Westminster
Ferry Terminal (P)
Temple
Blackfriars
Waterloo
Waterloo East
Southwark
Lambeth
Lambeth North
Kennington
VICTORIA EMBANKMENT
WESTMINSTER BRIDGE ROAD
LAMBETH PALACE ROAD
ALBERT EMBANKMENT
KENNINGTON ROAD
BLACKFRIARS ROAD
WATERLOO ROAD
STAMFORD STREET
UPPER GROUND
THE CUT
HORSEFERRY ROAD
MILLBANK
LAMBETH ROAD
ST GEORGE'S ROAD
BLACK PRINCE ROAD
KENNINGTON LA
HORSE GUARDS AVENUE
NORTHUMBERLAND AVENUE
WILLIAM IV STREET
KINGSWAY TUNNEL
Museum
Art Gallery
Education Facility
Hospital
Library
Police Station
Sports/Leisure Centre
1
2
3
4
5
6
7
8
9
10
11
12
13
14
15
16
17
18
19
20
21
22
23
24
25
26
27
28
29
30
31
32
33
34
35
36

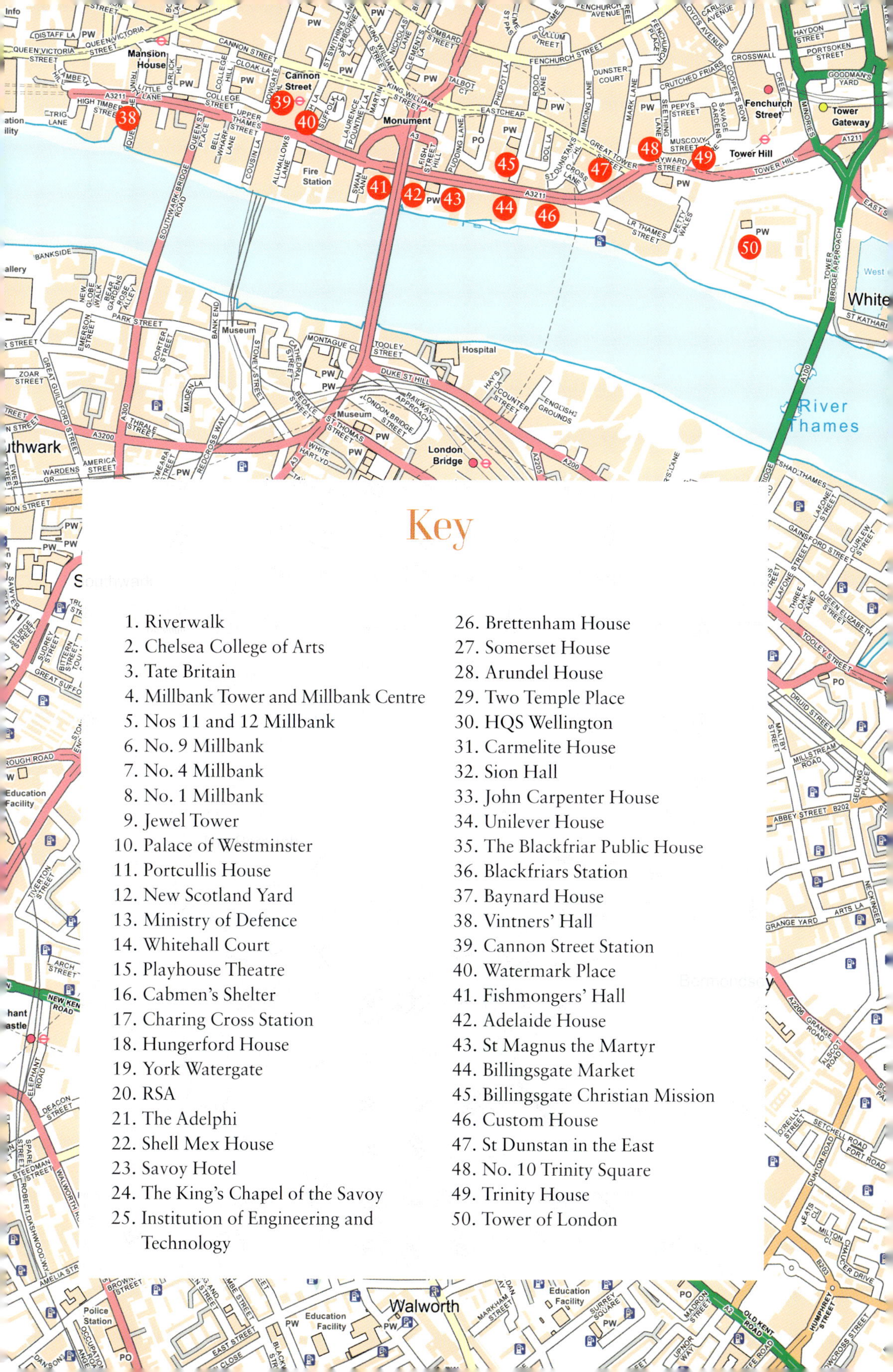

Key

1. Riverwalk
2. Chelsea College of Arts
3. Tate Britain
4. Millbank Tower and Millbank Centre
5. Nos 11 and 12 Millbank
6. No. 9 Millbank
7. No. 4 Millbank
8. No. 1 Millbank
9. Jewel Tower
10. Palace of Westminster
11. Portcullis House
12. New Scotland Yard
13. Ministry of Defence
14. Whitehall Court
15. Playhouse Theatre
16. Cabmen's Shelter
17. Charing Cross Station
18. Hungerford House
19. York Watergate
20. RSA
21. The Adelphi
22. Shell Mex House
23. Savoy Hotel
24. The King's Chapel of the Savoy
25. Institution of Engineering and Technology
26. Brettenham House
27. Somerset House
28. Arundel House
29. Two Temple Place
30. HQS Wellington
31. Carmelite House
32. Sion Hall
33. John Carpenter House
34. Unilever House
35. The Blackfriar Public House
36. Blackfriars Station
37. Baynard House
38. Vintners' Hall
39. Cannon Street Station
40. Watermark Place
41. Fishmongers' Hall
42. Adelaide House
43. St Magnus the Martyr
44. Billingsgate Market
45. Billingsgate Christian Mission
46. Custom House
47. St Dunstan in the East
48. No. 10 Trinity Square
49. Trinity House
50. Tower of London

A Welcome from the Authors

London's North Bank in 50 Buildings encompasses the area along the north side of the Thames stretching from Pimlico in the west to the Tower of London in the east. As with our previous book, *London's South Bank in 50 Buildings*, it is written imagining you are undertaking this walk virtually or on foot, and in stages or all in one go.

Starting at the boundary of Pimlico, next to Victoria, the first building in the book, Riverwalk, is also the newest, its flowing lines emulating the river it overlooks. Yet very quickly you find yourself passing far older structures with fascinating histories, such as the former Royal Army Medical Corps barracks and Tate Britain, both built on the site of the notorious Millbank Prison.

The walk eastwards to a pivotal point, the 'Westminster Bubble', takes you past iconic modern architecture to commercial HQs adorned with eye-catching statuary and reliefs, now repurposed as government buildings and apartments. While the Palace of Westminster area is usually hectic and full of visitors, before and beyond this point the North Bank is surprisingly tranquil. Thanks to the imagination of Joseph Bazalgette, the wide boulevard of the Embankment provides a pleasant walk beyond Westminster, even more so when strolling through the open spaces and gardens. It is ironic that Bankside and the pre-Second World War industrial area around Waterloo on the south side, regarded for centuries as relatively unimportant, are today buzzing with more visitors than the north side of the Thames.

Towards Blackfriars the character of the North Bank changes again. This is no surprise as it is here that you leave the City of Westminster and enter the 'Square Mile', officially the City of London, as signalled by one of the fierce City dragons you pass on the Embankment, marking the boundary.

The City has many wonderful and charming alleyways and courtyards, but by following the Thames Path you are rewarded with superb views of many buildings profiled in this book, with the added bonus of views across to buildings featured in *London's South Bank in 50 Buildings*. Taking both volumes will enable you to make the most of your North Bank journey.

Within the Square Mile you delve much further back into Britain's history, with buildings linking to London life, places of worship, education and trades and to its wider role in the management of the country such as administering the docks, collecting customs duties and protection of the coast.

We recognise that 'our' chosen fifty buildings may not be 'yours', but we do promise new discoveries alongside familiar favourites, and by the time you reach the Tower of London you will have traced the development of Britain's role in trade, industry, exploration, art, science, public hygiene, education, transport and, above all, architecture.

Louis Berk and Rachel Kolsky

The 50 Buildings

1. Riverwalk

Occupying a commanding position at the north end of Vauxhall Bridge and facing the iconic MI6 building, Riverwalk is a stunning apartment block. Completed in 2015, architects Stanton Williams designed an eye-catching curvaceous exterior inspired by the waves of the tidal Thames alongside.

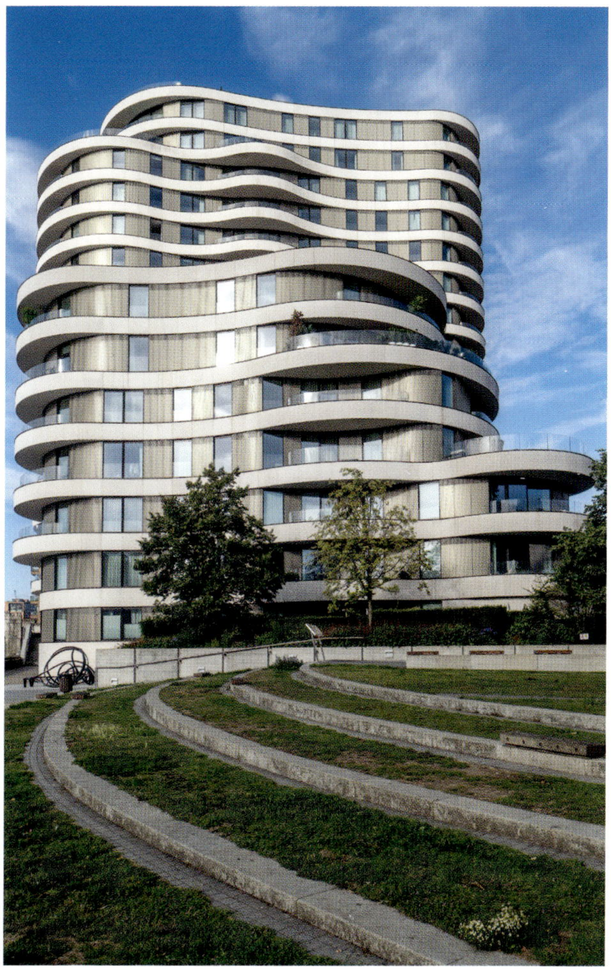

Riverwalk.

Linked by a lobby, two blocks of six and sixteen storeys house 116 apartments of various sizes plus a residents-only gym and public café. Separate affordable housing, required for specific new developments, is located nearby.

The building materials – Portuguese stone and bronzed aluminium – complement Ponsonby Terrace to the north, and the metal and glass façade represent geological bands of limestone. Stepped upper floors, incorporating sinuous penthouse terraces, have been designed to ensure unimpeded views of the Palace of Westminster (see Entry 10).

Riverside Walk Gardens was originally landscaped as a mini-park in the late 1960s/early 1970s after the embankment was cleared of light industry, notably ship-breaking yards. In 1968 Henry Moore's 1963–64 *Locking Piece* was installed.

The Riverwalk project re-landscaped and widened this open space, retaining public access along the river forming the perfect entry point for walking London's North Bank. Two artworks commissioned in 2016 from the Paris-based Argentine artist Pablo Reinoso are fashioned from black steel in the form of shaped public benches harmonising with both Riverwalk and the Thames. One, *Only Children*, encourages use of the area for play, while *We Watch You Too* is a light-hearted reference to MI6 opposite.

Address: No. 161 Millbank, SW1P 4FA
Built: 2015
Public Access: Café only
Tube: Pimlico

2. Chelsea College of Arts

Following the closure of Millbank Penitentiary (see Box) on this site in 1890, buildings for two military medical organisations were erected: the Queen Alexandra Military Hospital (QAMH), opened in 1905 by King Edward VII and Queen Alexandra, and the Royal Army Medical College (RAMC) HQ, opened two years later by Alexandra. An officers' mess and residential accommodation were built alongside. Alexandra had supported nursing and medical initiatives since 1863 when she married Edward, then Prince of Wales. The QAMH wards were named after RAMC holders of the Victoria Cross, a very suitable linkage.

Four buildings designed by John Henry Townsend Wood and Wilfred Ainslie surround what was the parade ground. The style they chose became known as Edwardian or Imperial Baroque, characterised by exterior detailing with red brick, stucco work and ornate stone reliefs, while interiors would incorporate elaborate decoration with swags and panelling. The mess and residential accommodation are more reminiscent of French Renaissance. During the First World War the RAMC became a hospital, producing typhoid vaccines and, despite Second World War damage, thousands of army medical personnel underwent tropical medicine training there. Postwar, facilities continued to expand, with 300 beds by 1957. The QAMH transferred to Woolwich in 1977 and in 2005 the RAMC relocated to Cosham, near Portsmouth. By then, several blocks had already been demolished making way for extensions to Tate Britain (see Entry 3).

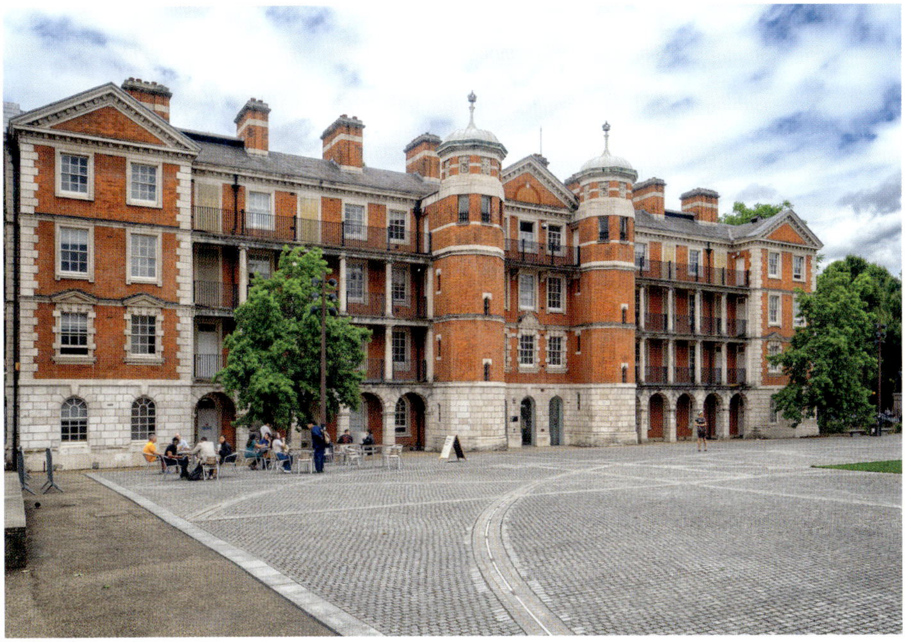

Above and below left: Chelsea College of Arts.

Below right: Millbank Prison Bollard.

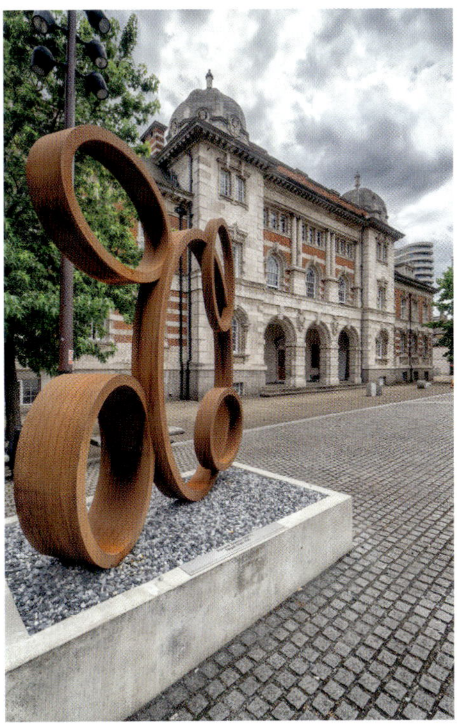

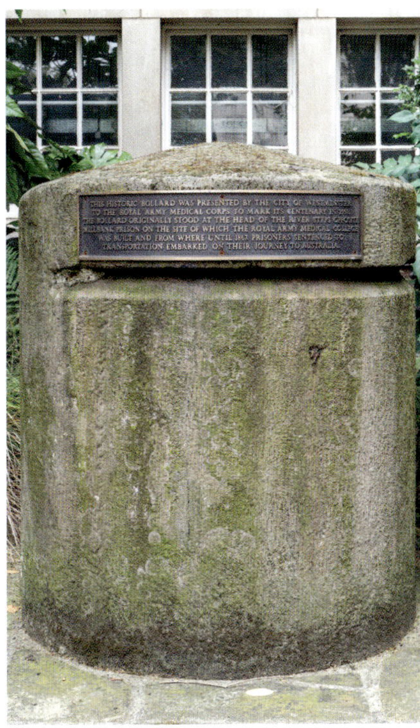

In 2000 the London Institute acquired the site from the Ministry of Defence (see Entry 13) for Chelsea College of Arts. With courses including fine art, graphic design and textile studies, Chelsea has an annual intake of over 1,400 students, with the parade ground showcasing ever-changing student exhibits alongside surviving plinths from Millbank Penitentiary.

Address: No. 16 John Islip Street, SW1P 4JU
Built: 1907
Listed Status: Grade II (except QAMH buildings)
Public Access: No
Tube: Pimlico
Website: arts.ac.uk

Millbank Prison

The name Millbank derives from a fourteenth-century mill owned by Westminster Abbey and its earth banks constructed to prevent flooding, but more latterly is associated either with anonymous government buildings or the infamous Millbank Penitentiary. Two plinths mark the spot where the prison existed from 1816 until closing in 1890. Designed as a panopticon, a small number of wardens could administer nearly 1,500 inmates. By 1903 the prison had been totally demolished, with the site later used for the Tate Gallery and RAMC (see Entries 2, 3).

3. Tate Britain

This site, originally part of Millbank Penitentiary (see Box), was acquired for the National Gallery of British Art and opened as the Tate Gallery in 1897. Designed by Sidney Smith, its grand porticoed entrance is fronted by six Corinthian columns with art-themed angel reliefs above the doorway. Atop the pediment sits Britannia flanked by a lion and a unicorn, reflecting that the collection has housed British art from 1545 to the present day – twentieth-century European art moved to Tate Modern on Bankside in 2000.

The entrance leads to a rotunda, which underwent considerable restoration between 2012 and 2013 as part of the mammoth Millbank Project that began in 2007. Under the direction of architect firm Caruso St John, it incorporates original Smith decorations including clamshell motifs and alcoves for displaying artworks.

Opening with eight rooms and 245 artworks, gallery space doubled with the 1906 extension. Among the collection's treasures are pieces by Millais, Moore, Lowry, Bacon and, famously, Turner, who bequeathed 300 paintings and 30,000 sketches. Displayed originally in a 1910 purpose-built wing, they are currently housed in the Clore Gallery, designed by James Stirling and completed in 1986. Turner is depicted on the current £20 banknotes, referencing a 1799 self-portrait in the collection and Caruso's rotunda staircase.

The demolition of the Queen Alexandra Military Hospital (QAMH) (see Entry 2) created space for subsequent extensions including two galleries from 1937, each over 90 metres long. Known as 'The Duveens' after their art-dealing funder, they were designed for displaying sculptures. Another gallery was added in 1979, followed by the Clore extension in 1986.

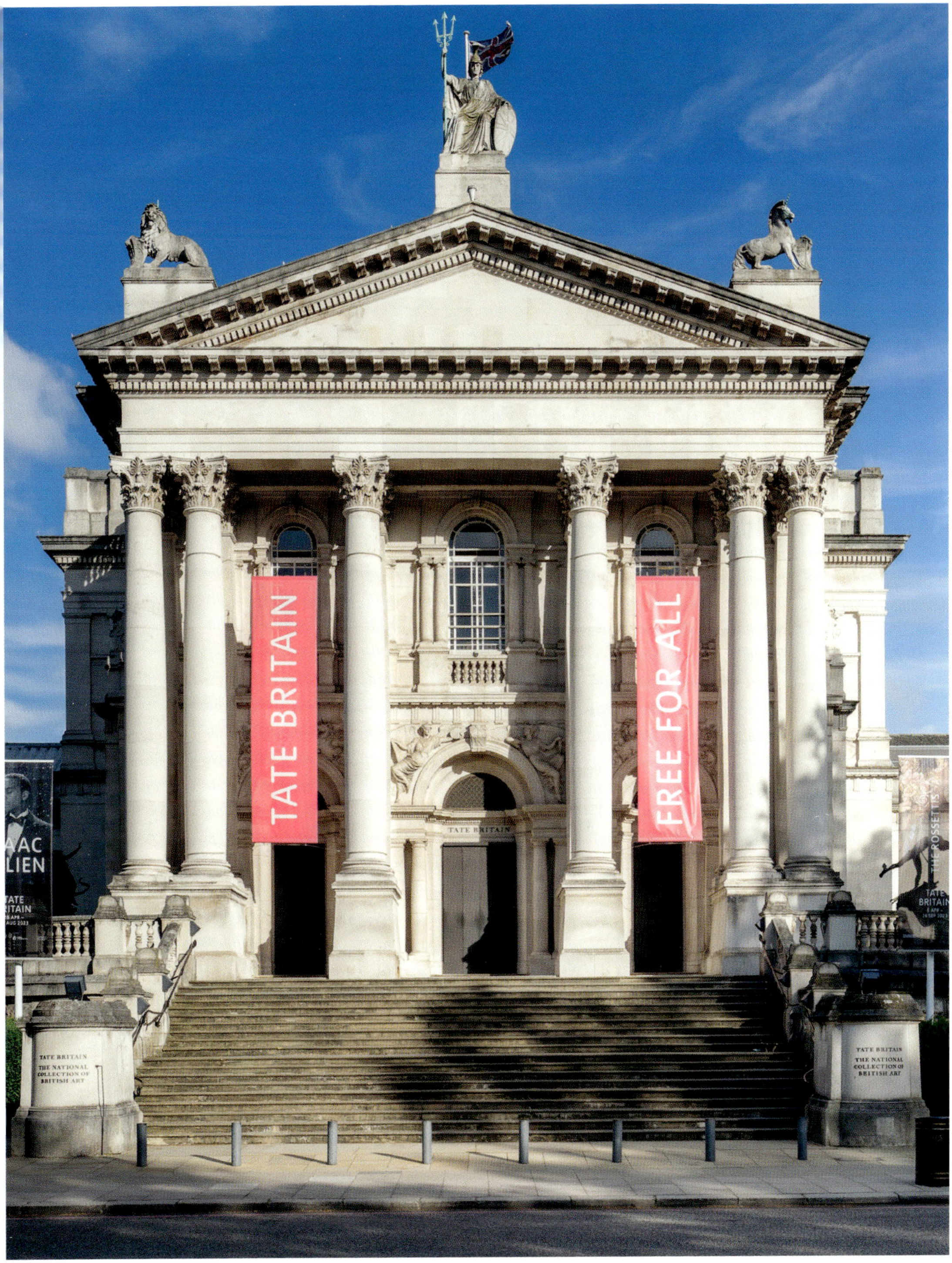

Tate Britain.

The surviving QAMH red-brick lodge is currently the director's offices, with gates retaining the initials 'QA'.

The name Tate commemorates Henry Tate, arts benefactor and founder of the gallery who also funded free libraries, including several in south London where he resided.

His successful sugar-refining company merged with a syrup manufacturer in 1926, forming Tate & Lyle.

Address: Millbank, SW1P 4RG
Built: 1892–97; 1910, 1926, 1937, 1979, 1986 and 2007–13
Listed Status: Grade II*
Public Access: Yes
Tube: Pimlico
Website: tate.org.uk

4. Millbank Tower and Millbank Centre

Despite the Pevsner architectural guide description 'worthy of affection' and RIBA (Royal Institute of British Architects) deeming it elegant and distinctive, Millbank Tower, with its neighbour the Millbank Centre, has for decades been one of London's least appreciated buildings – its sheer size out of proportion to the skyline.

Designed by Roland Ward & Partners and completed in 1963, its thirty-two floors reach 118 metres in height. Until 1965, when the Post Office Tower was built, it was London's tallest building, but it still dominates the North Bank west of Lambeth Bridge. Starting life as Vickers Tower, being built for engineering and chemical firms Vickers and ICI (see Entries 5, 6), the name references the geographic position. Its first function now forgotten, an original Vickers boardroom has been retained.

The reinforced concrete central core is surrounded by glass curtain walls with stainless-steel mullions separating opaque blue glass windows. The lower-level plinth on which the tower stands merits attention, with visitors entranced by sinuous convex and concave sides surrounding a small courtyard leading to a Y-shaped office block. Staircases – with no public access – lead to upper levels.

Outside the main entrance stands *Momentum III* by Michael Speller, an elongated figure in motion, typical of his style.

With Vickers and ICI long departed, the building is best remembered as home to various organisations, including the Labour Party, Conservative Party and United Nations. Since 2002, it has been owned by property magnates the Reuben brothers and leased to several smaller commercial and charitable bodies. Substantial redevelopment to John McAslan designs is due to break ground in 2024 and will include a 150-room five-star hotel in the Y-shaped block alongside 207 luxury apartments in the tower.

Address: Nos 21–24 Millbank, SW1P 4QP
Built: 1963
Listed Status: Grade II
Public Access: No
Tube: Pimlico

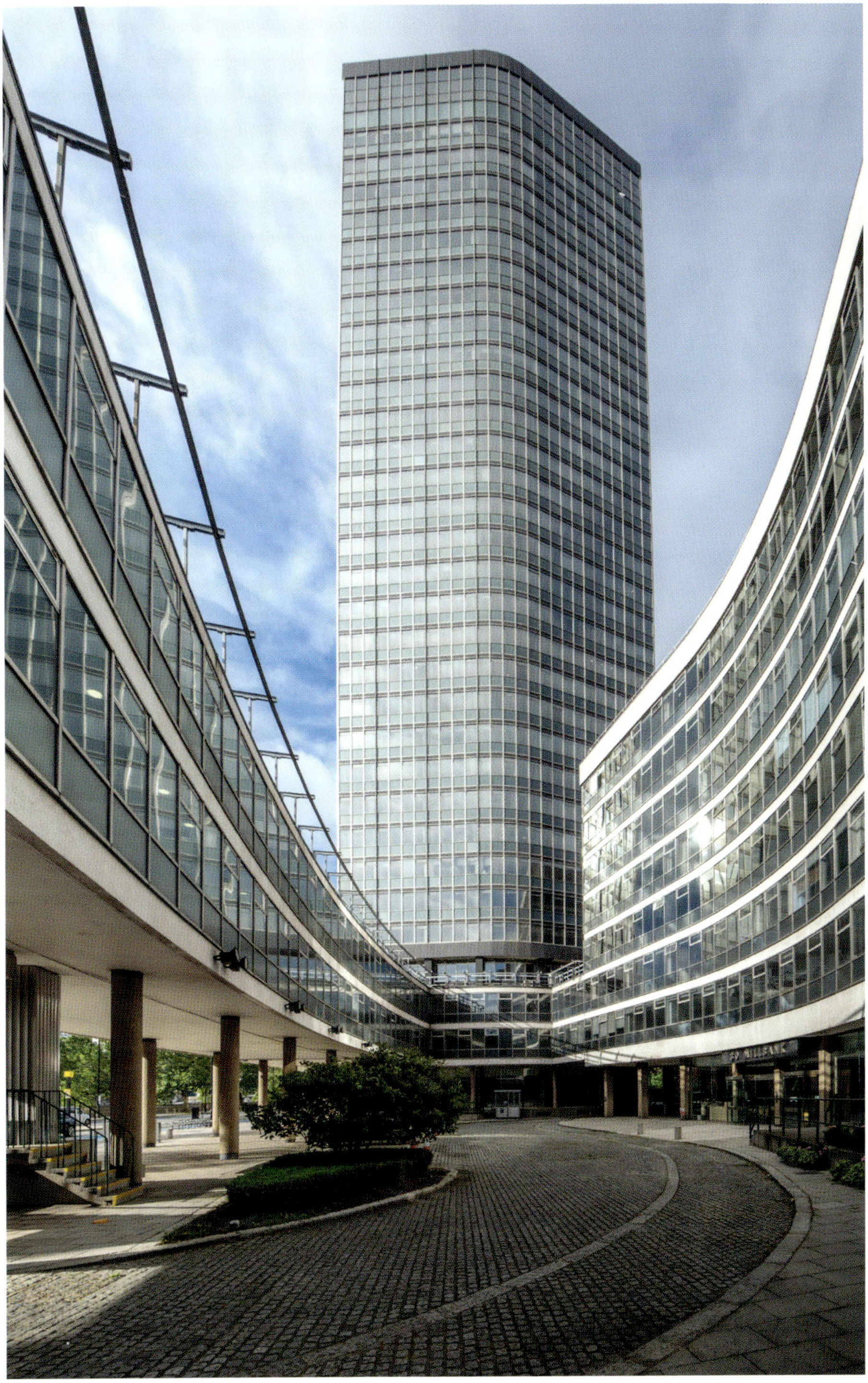

Millbank Tower and Millbank Centre.

5. Nos 11 and 12 Millbank

Thames House, together with Nobel House (see Entry 6), was designed by the government's chief architect, Sir Frank Baines, for Imperial Chemical Industries (ICI) and completed in 1930.

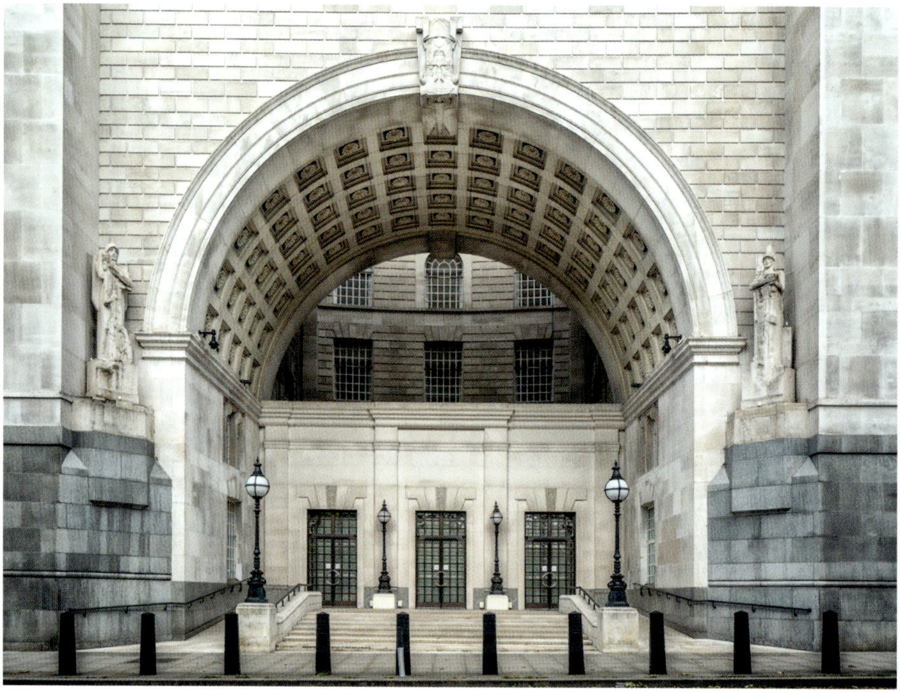

Above and below: Nos 11 and 12 Millbank.

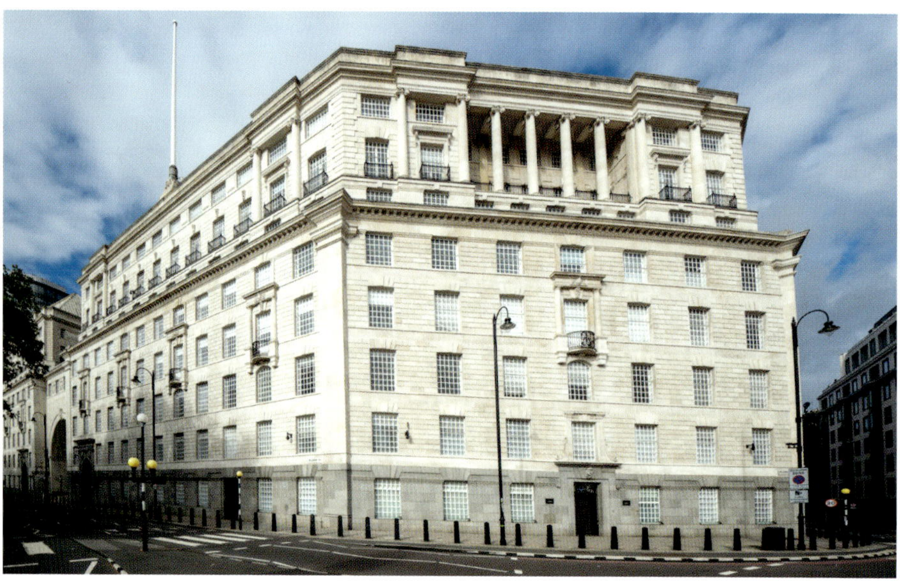

ICI evolved from several companies run by the German Mond family following Ludwig Mond's arrival in the UK in 1862. He collaborated with John Brunner, forming Brunner-Mond, and in 1926 Mond's son Alfred consolidated various Mond firms into ICI.

The timing of the building's construction is linked to Millbank's less salubrious past. The area was prone to flooding, and following the disastrous floods of 1928 when fourteen people died the opportunity was taken to demolish densely packed streets of working-class housing and redevelop the site for ICI offices, its position close to the Palace of Westminster (see Entry 10), reflecting its wealth and prestige.

Its neoclassical exterior is embellished with sculptural reliefs by Charles Sargeant Jagger (see Entry 6), who, following the First World War service in the Artists Rifles, specialised in war memorials. Here he represents St. George and Britannia, both with swords.

The building is fronted by a dramatic arch leading to three tall entrance doors. The keystone holds a variety of symbols including a bearded, blindfolded man who bears a set of scales and a sword, perhaps representing justice. The man appears above a smaller entrance, this time with dolphins, and a long-haired maiden above another entrance wears a delightful shell headdress. Other headwear on keystones includes crowns and men's caps, but careful scrutiny of the exterior will also reveal seafaring items such as oars, hooks, sails and mooring rings.

During the 1980s the government acquired the building, which has since been home to MI5, the UK's Security Service. It was extensively refurbished in the 1990s and reopened by the then Prime Minister, John Major.

Address: Nos 11–12 Millbank, SW1P 4QP
Built: 1928
Listed Status: Grade II
Public Access: No
Tube: Pimlico

6. No. 9 Millbank

Decorated reliefs on the vast Portland stone frontage at No. 9 Millbank provide clues to its original purpose. Designed as an office block for ICI (see Entries 4, 5) by Sir Frank Baines, designer of Thames House, it was completed in 1931 as Imperial Chemicals House. At a time of great advances in construction techniques it was built swiftly, incorporating innovations, seen also in large department stores of the time, such as electric lighting and ozone air. Inside, doors and panelling of Austrian oak were set into marble-lined walls.

At fifth-floor level, stone engravings portray Ludwig and Alfred Mond by William Bateman Fagan alongside other notable chemists he sculpted, including Joseph Priestley and Alfred Nobel, who initiated the annual Nobel Prizes and whose name is given to the building next door (see Entry 5).

The same floor is decorated with statues designed by Charles Sargeant Jagger (see Entry 5), representing workers in chemicals, building, shipping and agriculture. The detail is astonishing, down to hobnailed boots, rippling muscles, bare arms and expressions of intense concentration.

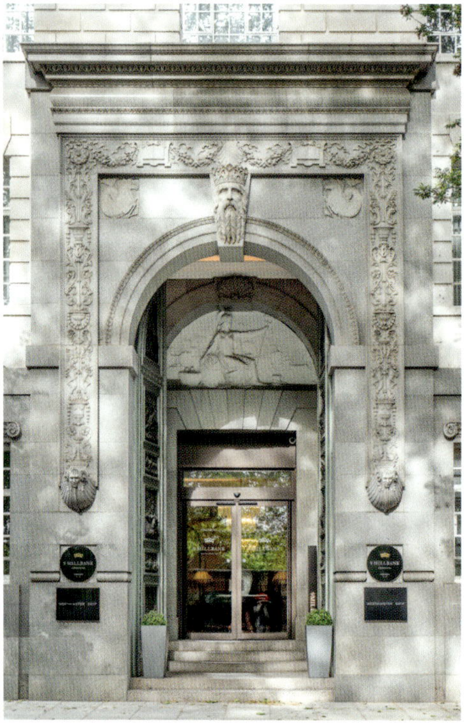

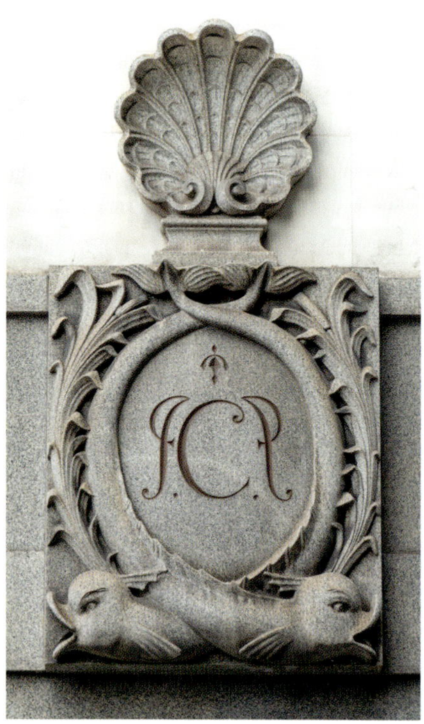

Above and below: No. 9 Millbank.

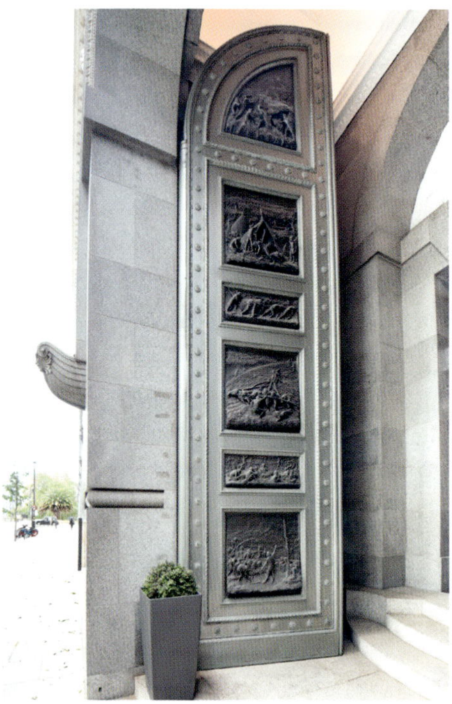

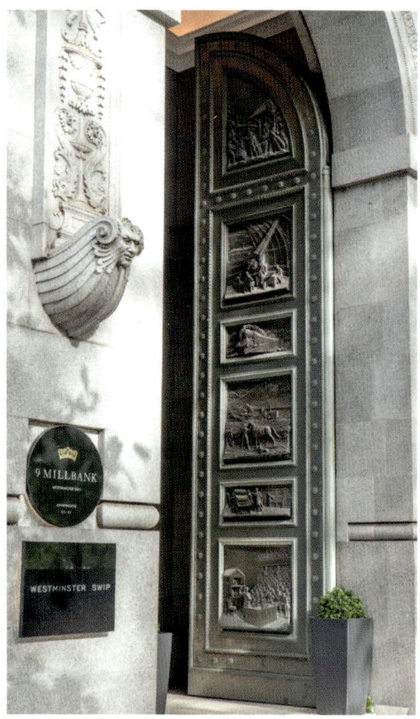

Two magnificent 6-metre-high bronze entrance doors designed by Fagan in 1927 are decorated with intricate reliefs portraying scientific and technical progress, with hunting, housing and agriculture on the left and, to the right, science-related innovation including astronomy, transport, Faraday (see Entries 25, 49) and Jacquard looms with clog-wearing factory workers. Granite reliefs surrounding the doorway depict shipping.

Several ICI initials are dotted around the exterior, together with the date 1928 – when building commenced.

During the twentieth century ICI diversified and expanded, with its pharmaceutical and chemical businesses eventually sold off. Now requiring smaller premises, it was divided in 1987 forming Norwest House and subsequently No. 9 Millbank and Nobel House. When ICI moved out in the 1990s, Eric Parry Architects refurbished and converted the block into 177 luxury homes, preserving ICI boardrooms and directors' offices on the upper floors as five heritage homes.

There is no public access despite the vast entrance doors always tantalisingly left open.

Address: No. 9 Millbank, SW1P 3GE
Built: 1928–31; refurbishment 2022
Listed Status: Grade II
Public Access: No
Tube: Pimlico

7. No. 4 Millbank

Designed in neoclassical style by John W. Simpson and Maxwell Ayrton, architects of the iconic 1923 Wembley Stadium, the corner building at Great Peter Street with its external walls of Portland stone is a further example of the large office blocks built along Millbank during the early 1900s.

The entrance is topped by two sculptures by Albert Hodge (see Entry 48), a woman sitting on an Ionic column and a man carrying a bundle of sticks and an axe, emblems typically representing authority and power. A small figurehead and a mooring ring indicate maritime travel, referencing the overseas associations of the building's original purpose.

It was constructed between 1914 and 1916 during the First World War as offices of the Crown Agents for the Colonies, which administered construction projects throughout what was then an extensive empire. The rapid development of railways, engineering, infrastructure projects and trade around the British Empire from the mid-nineteenth century necessitated considerable capital and also numerous staff, who from 1908 were accorded the status of civil servants.

By the First World War British colonies were on every continent, with over 400 million people comprising nearly a quarter of the world's population. As activity increased the agents moved from one rented property to another, eventually transferring to these purpose-built offices, the size and location, close to the Palace of Westminster (see Entry 10), reflecting its status.

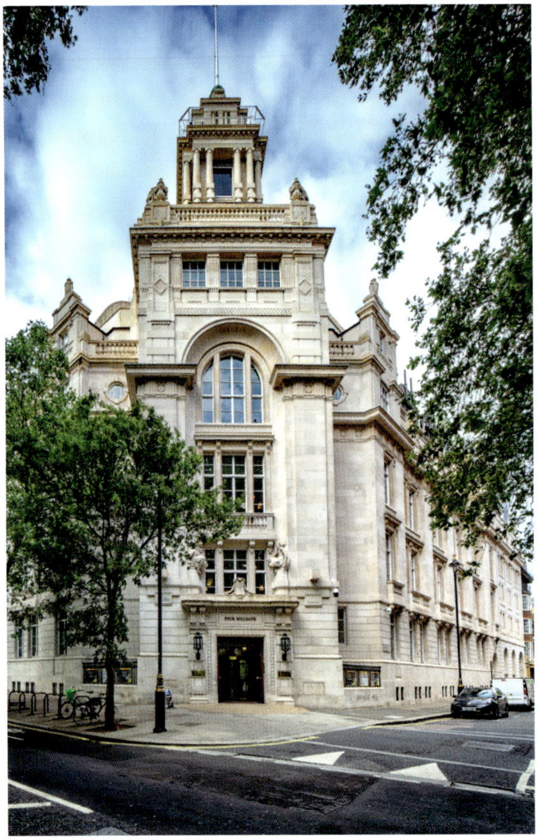

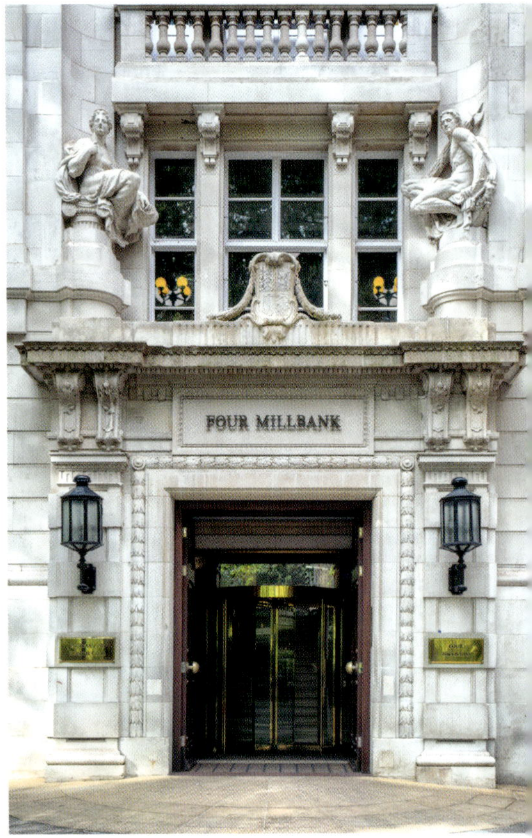

Above left and above right: No. 4 Millbank.

The agents relocated in 1986 to Sutton, subsequently becoming a not-for-profit international development company.

A Saudi Arabian property company refurbished the building in 1987. Stonework was cleaned, wooden window frames treated and the roof repaired using traditional copper detailing, with any new windows matching the originals. The building is now a multi-purpose block with offices, studios, venue spaces, apartments and a health club.

Inside, the grand staircase has been fully restored with a seven-storey-high lobby topped with a glass roof. A key tenant is the BBC, with studios for Parliamentary broadcasts opened by ex-Prime Minister Margaret Thatcher in 1991.

Address: No. 4 Millbank, SW1P 3LL
Built: 1916; renovated 1987–89
Listed Status: Grade II*
Public Access: Restaurant only
Tube: Pimlico, St. James's Park, Westminster
Website: fourmillbank.com

8. No. 1 Millbank

The building on the corner of Great College Street is easily missed as the local view is dominated by the Palace of Westminster (see Entry 10). Also known as Millbank House, No. 1 Millbank is currently offices for the House of Lords and certainly worth closer inspection.

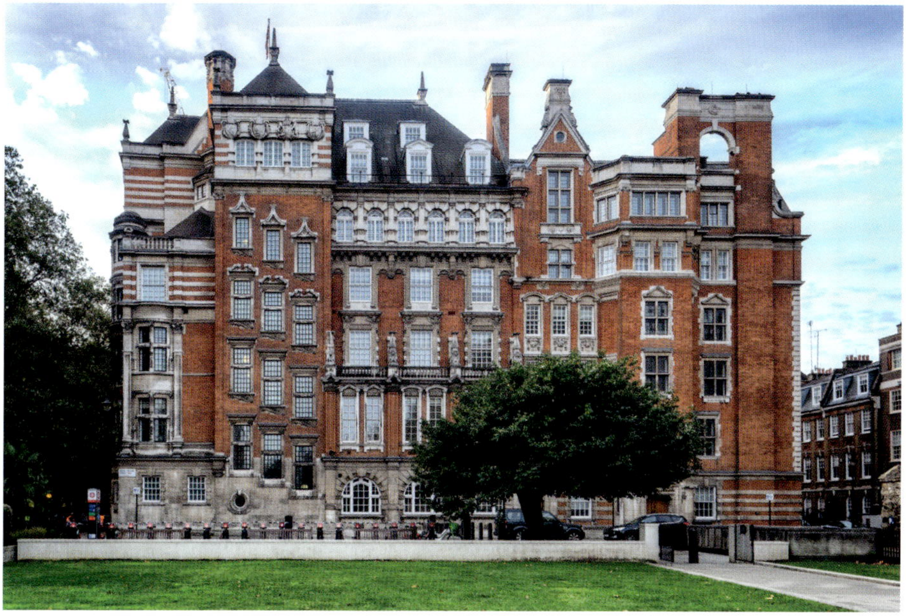

Above and below: No. 1 Millbank.

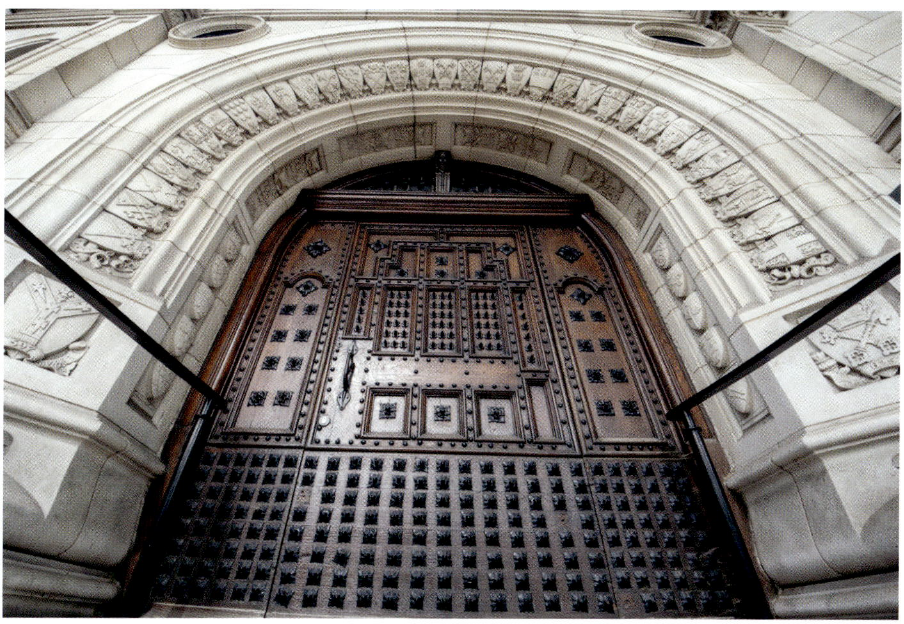

Constructed over several decades from the late nineteenth century and completed in 1930 to plans by W. D. Caröe, it comprises an island block of several red-brick buildings with Portland stone dressings, fronting four different streets but designed to complement each other. Classified by architectural critics as 'freestyle' Northern Renaissance, the detail includes windows of all shapes and sizes: long, wide, in a staircase formation, attic dormers and oriels, small towers, pinnacles and pediments – it is quite dazzling to the eye. The door, though usually open, looks at its most dramatic when closed, with eight rows of intimidating metal studs and additional studded panels above.

It is the entrance that provides a clue to the first occupants, the Church Commissioners – these were the Ecclesiastical Commission until 1948 when the latter merged with Queen Anne's Bounty, a 1704 charity supplementing the income of poor clergy. The doorway is framed by shields with city names and dates. Each represents a Church of England diocese and the year established. The earliest is London in AD 604, linking to the first church on the site of St Paul's Cathedral, while Bradford's with a wool sack and a pair of crossed keys is dated 1920. The arch incorporates undated rectangular reliefs, including Llandaff St Davids and British Lincoln.

The Church Commissioners is one of seven administrative bodies for the Church of England. Its role is to manage the Church's investment and property portfolios and fund projects within the Church and its communities. Since moving from No. 1 Millbank in 2005, it operates from Church House in Dean's Yard, Westminster Abbey.

Address: No. 1 Millbank, SW1P 4RP
Built: Late nineteenth century to 1930
Listed Status: Grade II*
Public Access: No
Tube: Westminster

9. Jewel Tower

Just four structures survived the devastating 1834 fire at the Palace of Westminster (see Entry 10). One is the Jewel Tower, set back from a small green opposite the House of Lords and instantly recognisable as the backdrop to regular TV political broadcasts filmed from the lawn.

Built in 1365 to store Edward III's treasures, this three-storey stone tower was originally known as the Privy Wardrobe but is now the perfect place to ponder the origin of words such as fathoms, firkins, quarts and pecks – measurements that have left regular conversation but crop up in pub names, as in The Fox and Firkin, or in proverbs such as 'Trying to fit a quart into a pint pot'.

The tower was originally part of a set of private premises for the monarch and his family but was separated from the palace by a moat on two sides. A spiral staircase led to the jewel keeper's accommodation, with other rooms used for storage including, from 1600, official and royal documents. Although a brick vault ensured they survived the fire, they were relocated to the newly built Victoria Tower in 1864. The Jewel Tower did not remain

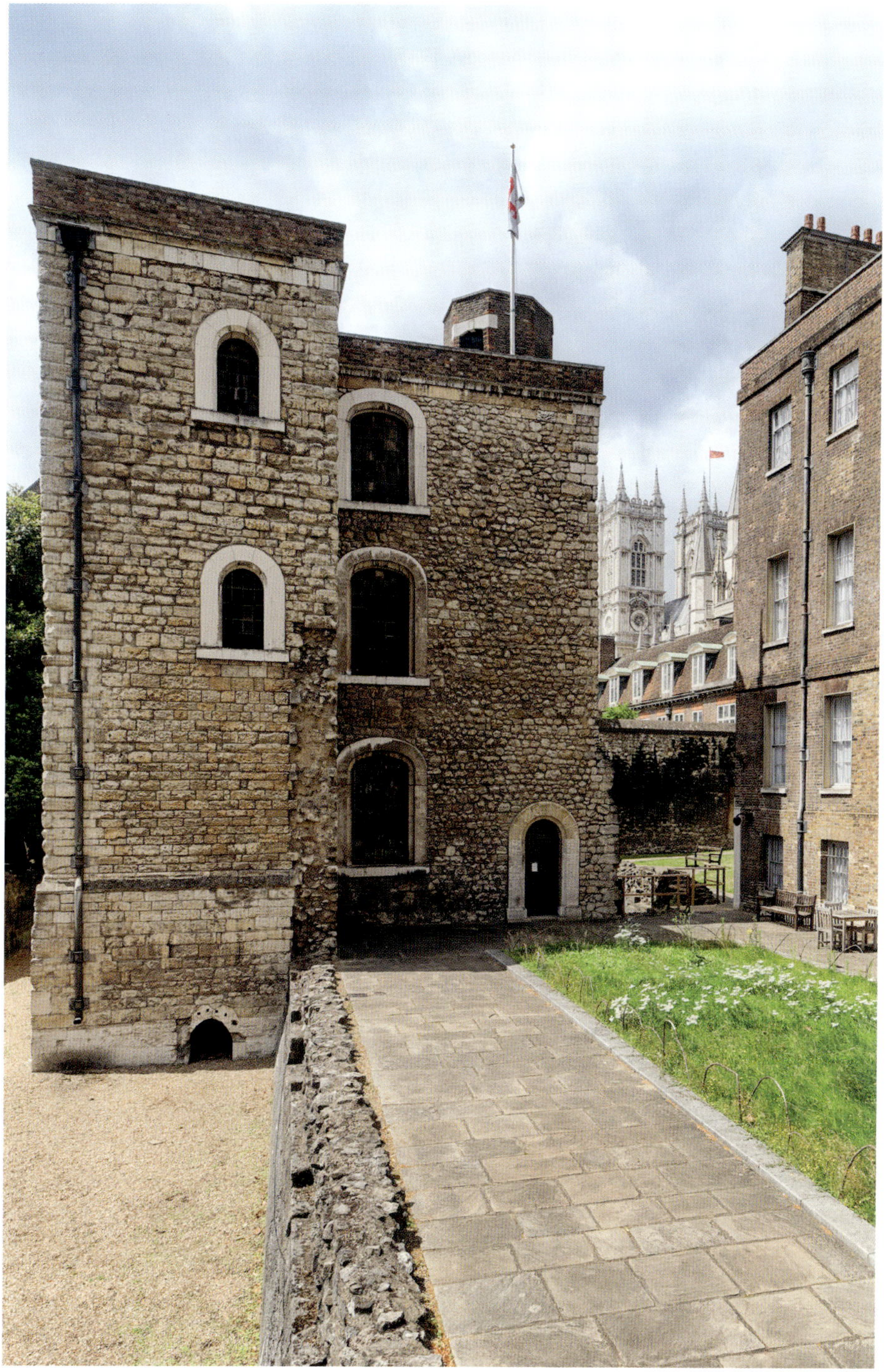

The Jewel Tower.

empty for long. In 1869 the Board of Trade Standards Department established its weights and measures teams here. Remaining until 1938, they moved to Teddington after increased traffic outside began to affect measurement accuracy. The moat, which by the mid-1600s was mostly blocked by debris, was refilled in 1963 but emptied in the 1990s due to poor drainage.

Although isolated from the pomp and pageantry of the Palace of Westminster, the tower with its fourteenth- and eighteenth-century vaults and lockable double doors showcases not only an important part of palace life but also stories behind the UK's curiously named weights and measures.

Address: Abingdon Street, SW1P 3JY
Built: 1365
Listed Status: Grade I
Public Access: Yes
Tube: Westminster
Website: english-heritage.org.uk

10. Palace of Westminster

The Gothic-style extravaganza of the Palace of Westminster dominates Parliament Square. Comprising the House of Commons and House of Lords, it is the workplace of 650 UK Members of Parliament (MPs) and 781 peers and diocesan bishops.

The original royal palace, dating from the eleventh century, gradually assumed importance as a law court and, later, the official seat of government. Almost totally destroyed by fire in 1834, only the Jewel Tower (see Entry 9), St Stephen's Chapter House, Cloister Court and Westminster Hall survived. The hall with its steep roof was completed in 1099 and is still used for ceremonial occasions, including the lying in state of Queen Elizabeth II prior to her funeral in September 2022.

The post-fire rebuilding competition was won by architect Charles Barry, with Augustus Pugin designing the decorative features and internal furnishings. Their chosen style was Victorian Gothic and emblems including the portcullis, fleur de lys and pomegranate feature heavily inside and out.

The Elizabeth Tower, with the clock, is better known as Big Ben (see Box). The central tower and spire is a ventilation shaft dispersing smoke from fireplaces and the western tower is the Victoria Tower. Housing the Parliamentary Archives, this is also the royal entrance.

The river frontage, *c.* 300 metres long, is best seen from the Albert Embankment. The balcony canopies in green and red and the paintwork of Westminster Bridge and Lambeth Bridge replicate the colours of the upholstery of the House of Commons and Lords respectively.

Following severe Second World War damage, the House of Commons was rebuilt to designs by Sir Giles Gilbert Scott, reopening in 1950. The 8 acres around the palace are designated a UNESCO World Heritage Site, but by the early twenty-first century the building, with its 1,100 rooms, 100 staircases and approximately 5 km of corridors,

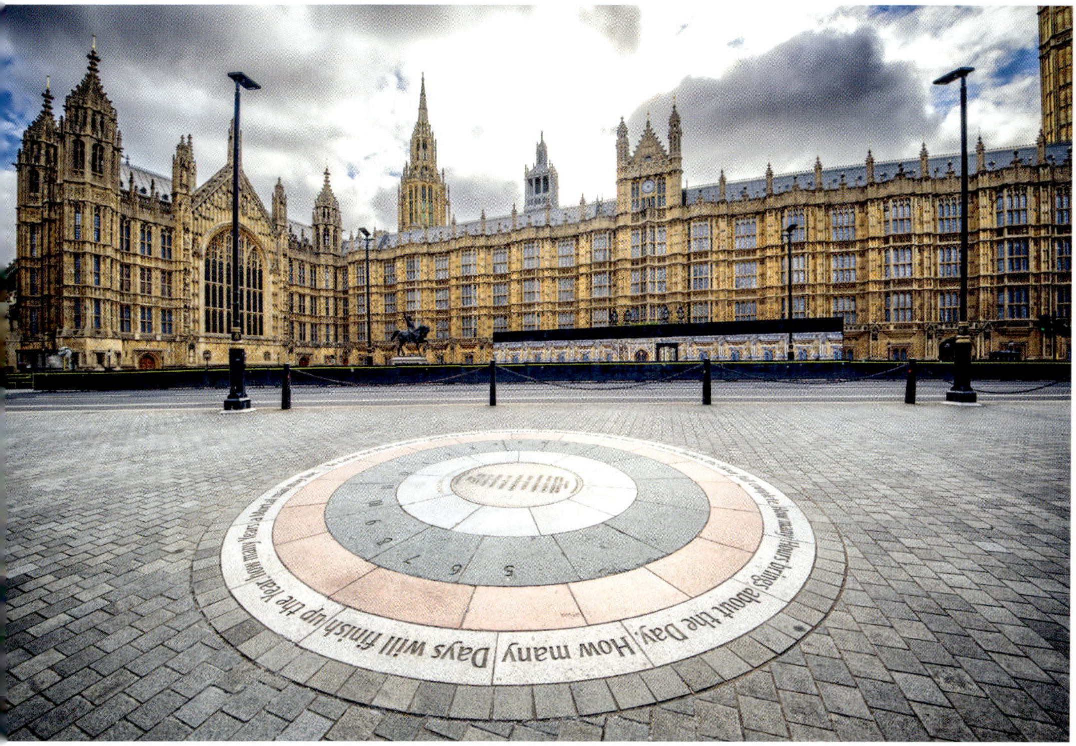

Above: The Palace of Westminster, from Old Palace Yard with Queen Elizabeth II Golden Jubilee sundial.

Below: The Palace of Westminster, from Albert Embankment.

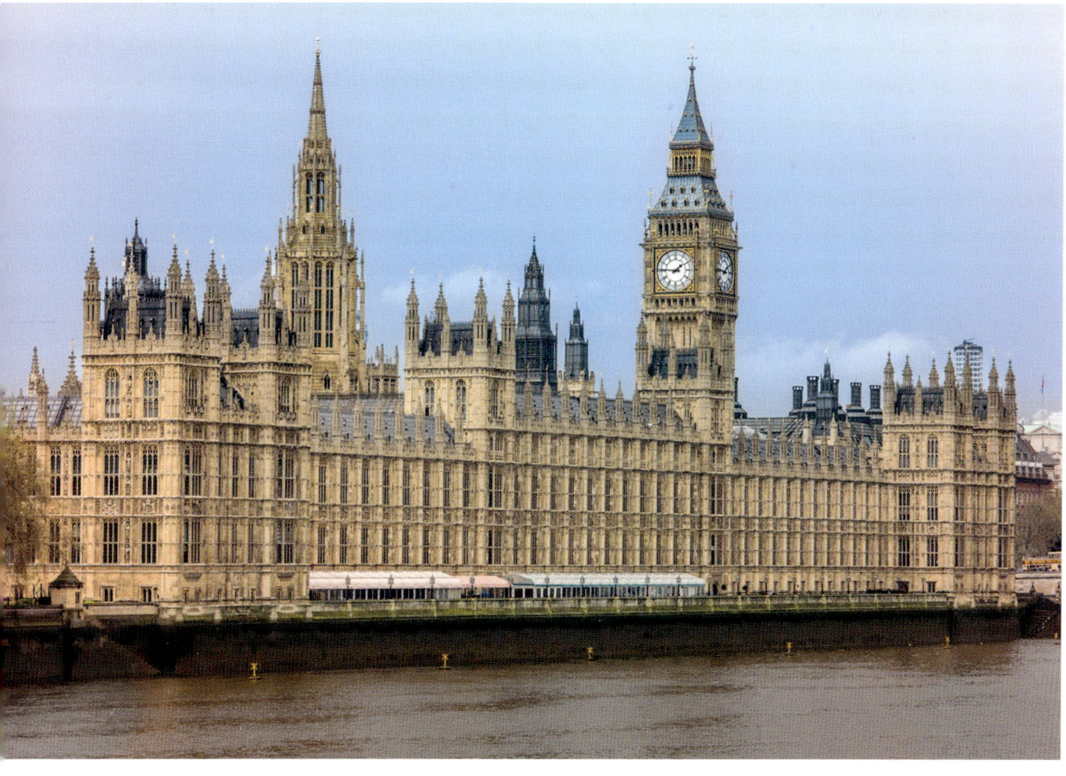

required considerable attention and a lengthy restoration and renewal programme began in 2013.

Address: London, SW1A 0AA
Built: 1838
Listed Status: Grade I
Public Access: Public tours
Tube: Westminster
Website: parliament.uk

Big Ben

The world's most recognised bell chimes are likely those of the Elizabeth Tower, nicknamed Big Ben. Originally St Stephen's Tower, it was renamed in 2012 commemorating Queen Elizabeth II's Diamond Jubilee. 'Big Ben' is actually the 13½-ton bell, reputedly named after Sir Benjamin Hall, the Commissioner of Works during construction. Striking the hours since 1859, it is accurate to one second and regulated with pre-decimal penny coins. Visitors can climb the 334 steps to experience the 'dongs' from behind the 7-metre square iron and glass clock face.

11. Portcullis House

The large rectangular office block facing Big Ben (see Box) is a homage in both design and the portcullis, one of the House of Commons (see Entry 10) emblems used extensively since the sixteenth century.

A 1980s audit of the Parliamentary estate identified the need for an additional 210 MP offices and select committee rooms. At the same time plans were underway for Jubilee Line access at Westminster station, providing the perfect opportunity for combining the two projects.

The corner site of Victorian buildings was cleared for the station and its seven-storey underground chamber. Above would be a freestanding block alongside the Norman Shaw Buildings (see Entry 12) with six vast columns, positioned as on a domino, supporting the inner courtyard from below.

Designed by Michael Hopkins, it was opened by Queen Elizabeth II in February 2001. The building incorporates an open arcade providing shelter for the Bridge Street and river frontages, along with entrances to the Tube and a row of shops. The distinctive roof line is topped with fourteen bronze-clad chimneys, complementing both those of the Norman Shaw Buildings and the Gothic pinnacles of the Palace of Westminster. They are of practical use too, as part of the air conditioning duct system.

Inside, the building opens into a courtyard with a glass roof at second-floor level supported by an intricate frame of intersected oak and steel beams. Oak is also the predominant material for furniture and panelling.

The double-storey internal cloister for committee rooms has public access via a glazed staircase with eateries, library and other facilities used by MPs visible to visitors passing

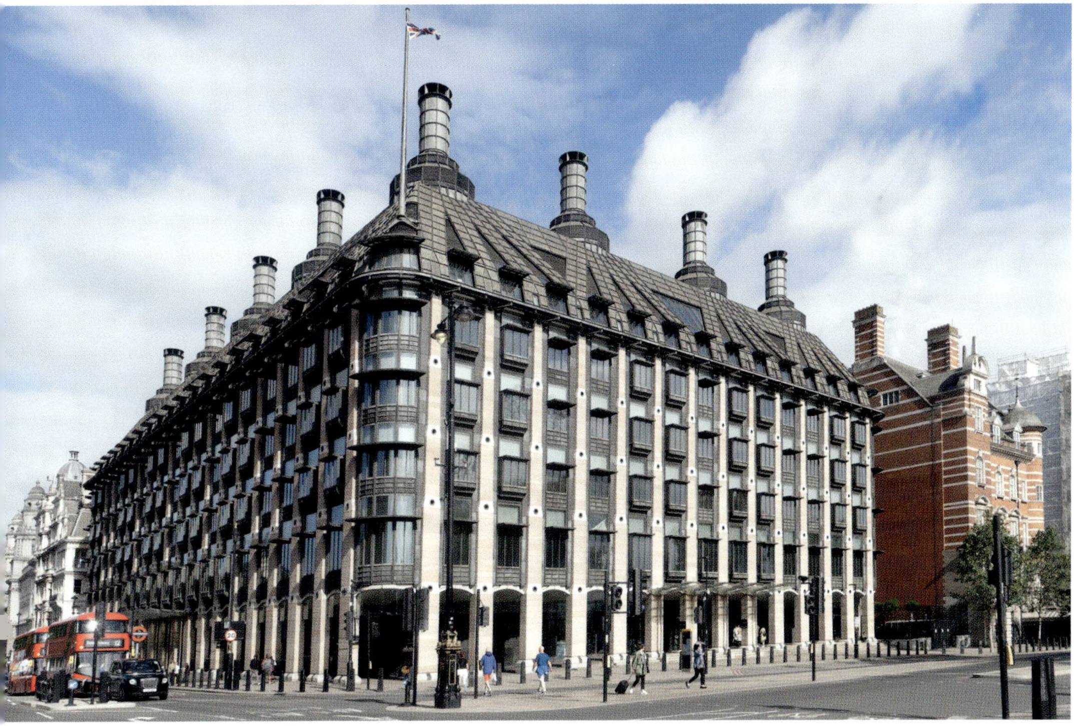

Above: Portcullis House.

Below left: Elizabeth Tower (Big Ben).

Below right: Norman Shaw Buildings.

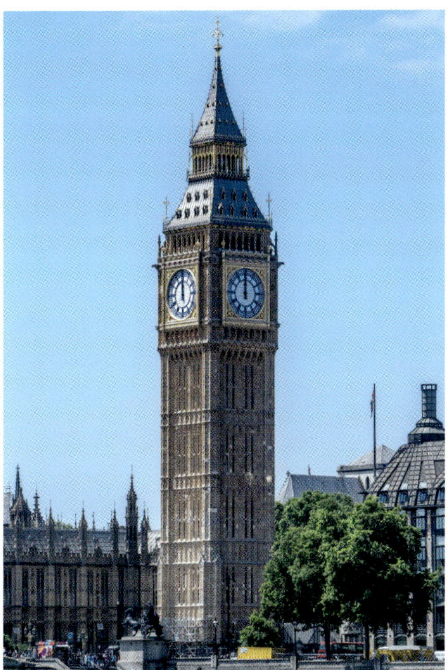

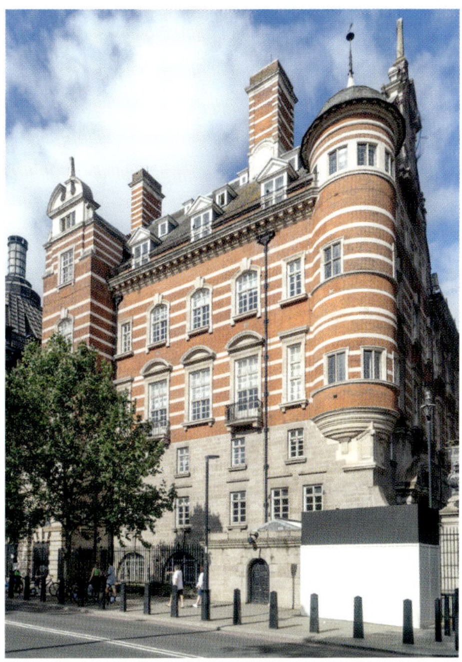

through. From the atrium, a subway provides the public entrance to Big Ben and a secure link to the Palace of Westminster.

Address: No. 1 Victoria Embankment, SW1A 2JR
Built: 1992–2001
Public Access: By appointment
Tube: Westminster

12. New Scotland Yard

Whitehall 1212 is one of the UK's most famous telephone numbers, instantly recognisable from when telephone exchange names were part of the number. Used from 1934 it connected to Scotland Yard, the nickname for London's Metropolitan Police (the Met) HQ, which has occupied four different sites. Today, two of these – the current and a previous – stand side by side.

The name Scotland Yard emerged around ten years after the Met was established by Robert Peel in 1829. The first commissioners occupied No. 4 Whitehall Place, which backed onto where the residence for the kings of Scotland once stood. The front entrance was on Whitehall, but the police station was at the back and thus nicknamed Scotland Yard.

The Met later moved to one of two adjacent purpose-built blocks on Victoria Embankment (see Box). Officially the Norman Shaw Buildings and named after their architect, they were nicknamed New Scotland Yard (NSY). The North block of 1890 and the South block built between 1902 and 1906 provided space for the rapidly expanding force. Linked by a bridge, both are in typical Norman Shaw Arts and Crafts design with colour-banded brickwork.

New Scotland Yard.

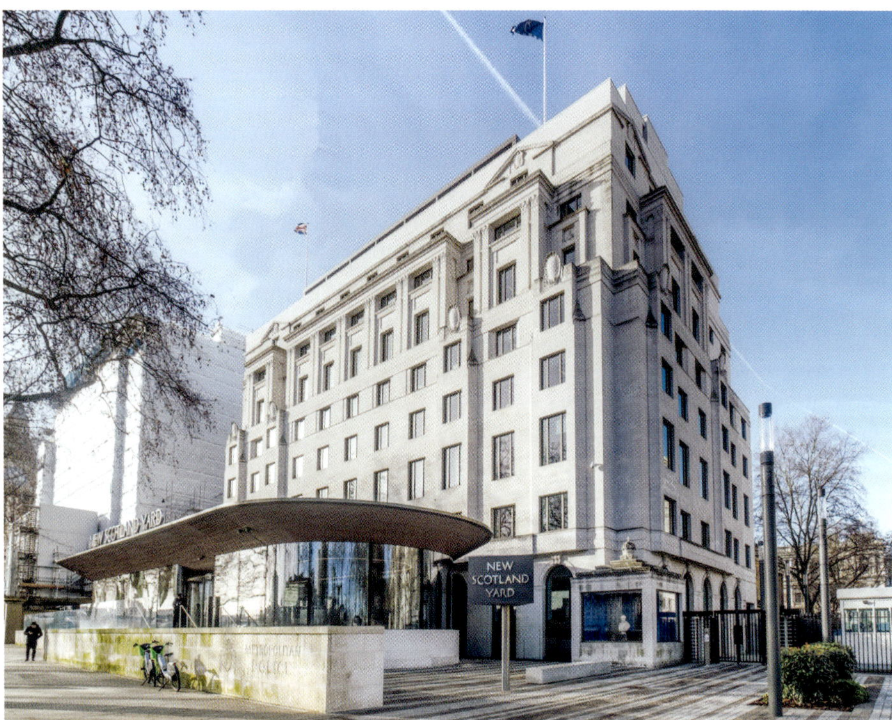

Shaw was assisted by John Dixon Butler, architect for the Met and designer of over 200 police stations and courthouses. Currently the blocks are home to Parliamentary offices.

The Met relocated to Victoria in 1967 but returned to the Whitehall area, occupying the 1930 Curtis Green (named after the architect) block, built originally as offices but refurbished between 2013 and 2016. Architects AHMM added a glazed pavilion entrance fronting the neoclassical Portland stone building, fulfilling the Met's brief for greater visibility, organisational transparency and public access.

The plinth on which it sits includes subtle stone banding, complementing the striped brickwork of the neighbouring Norman Shaw Buildings. The pavilion also functions as a memorial to police officers who died in the course of duty, with an eternal flame visible through the glass. The basement incorporates the Crime Museum, a collection based on an evidence archive gathered from the mid-1870s. Not open to the public, it is used for training and research purposes.

The iconic turning triangular sign from the 1960s NSY building has been incorporated at the front, ensuring a link on this short stretch of embankment to all three NSYs.

Address: Victoria Embankment, SW1A 2JF
Built: 1887–90, 1902–06; 1935–40 refurbished 2013–16
Listed Status: Grade I (Norman Shaw North), Grade II* (Norman Shaw South)
Public Access: Norman Shaw Buildings – No; New Scotland Yard foyer, memorial – Yes
Tube: Westminster
Website: met.police.uk

Battle of Britain Memorial

Unveiled in 2005, this memorial, a collaboration between Donald Insall Associates and sculptor Paul Day, commemorates the 1940 Battle of Britain, a pivotal Second World War air campaign. Cleverly built around a District line ventilation shaft, Day's sculpture incorporates details referencing the fighter planes, 2,936 pilot names, the crews, civilians looking skywards and the uniformed fighter bombers. Some emerge from the structure providing a sense of energy, power and courage vividly illustrating Churchill's famous quote about the battle: 'Never was so much owed by so many to so few.'

Battle of Britain Memorial.

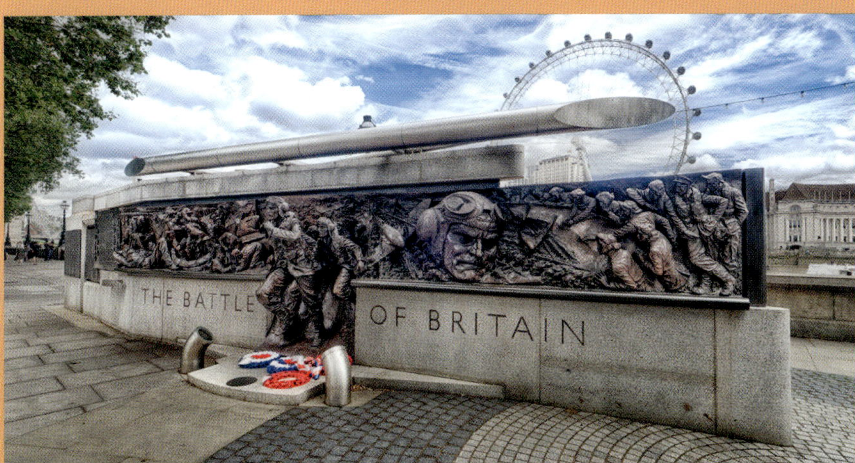

13. Ministry of Defence

Lying south of Whitehall, this enormous eight-storey Portland stone complex of the Ministry of Defence (MoD) extends 170 metres along the Victoria Embankment. An unequal rectangle, it stands on the site of what was Whitehall Palace, the main royal residence from 1530 until almost totally destroyed by fire in 1698.

The building evolved slowly. Designed by Vincent Harris in 1915, construction was delayed by the First World War, the interwar economic depression and the Second World War. In 1939 a small flight of stone steps was uncovered during the MoD construction. Designed by Sir Christopher Wren they were built in 1691 providing access to the Thames from the earlier palace.

When completed the MoD building consisted of four sections, each topped with a green copper roof and containing three internal courtyards, originally open to the sky.

The offices were first occupied in 1951 by the Board of Trade before the Air Ministry arrived in 1958. When the Air Ministry, Admiralty and War Office merged in 1964 to become the MoD, the new department required substantial office space and took over the complete building, with the Board of Trade relocating to Victoria Street.

There is little ornamentation, but above the Horse Guards Avenue entrance are two huge sculptures created in 1949 by Charles Wheeler. Resembling reclining 'Rubenesque' goddesses, each weighing 40 tons, *Earth* sits on a block of stone and wavy lines decorate *Water*. Emblems for the Royal Air Force, an eagle and crown, remain in situ carved on columns flanking the southern entrance.

Ministry of Defence.

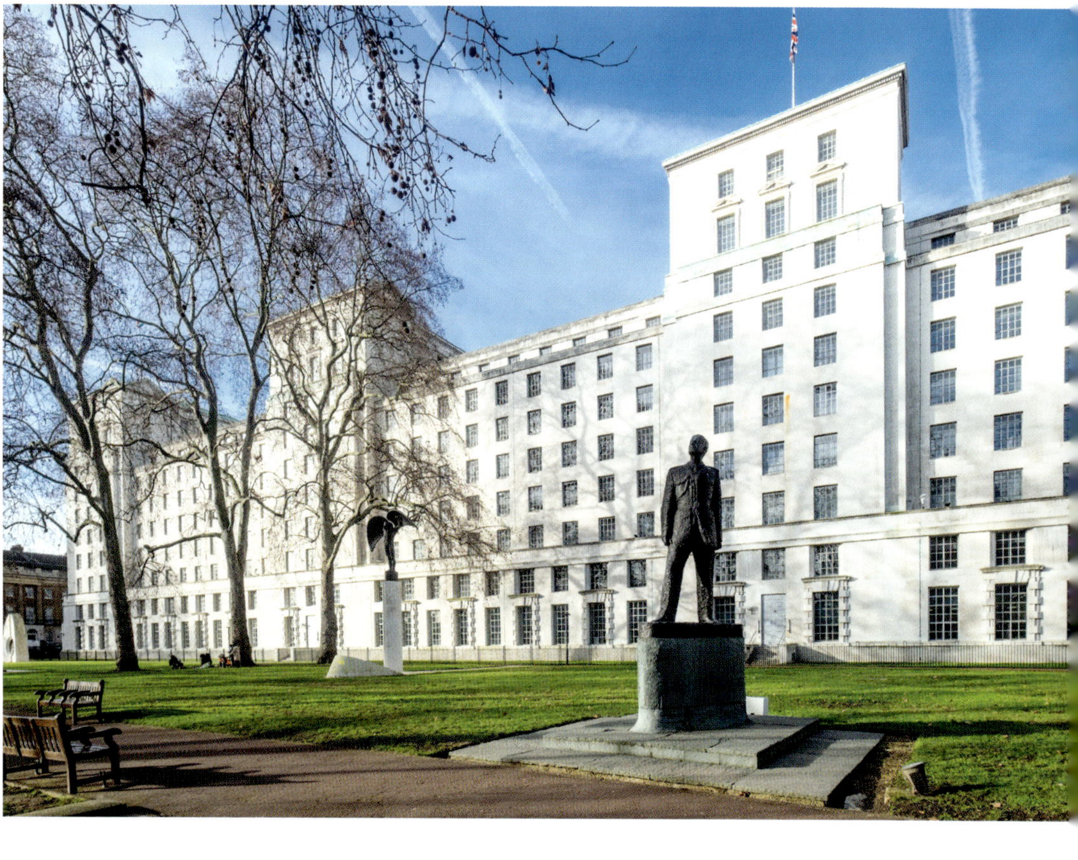

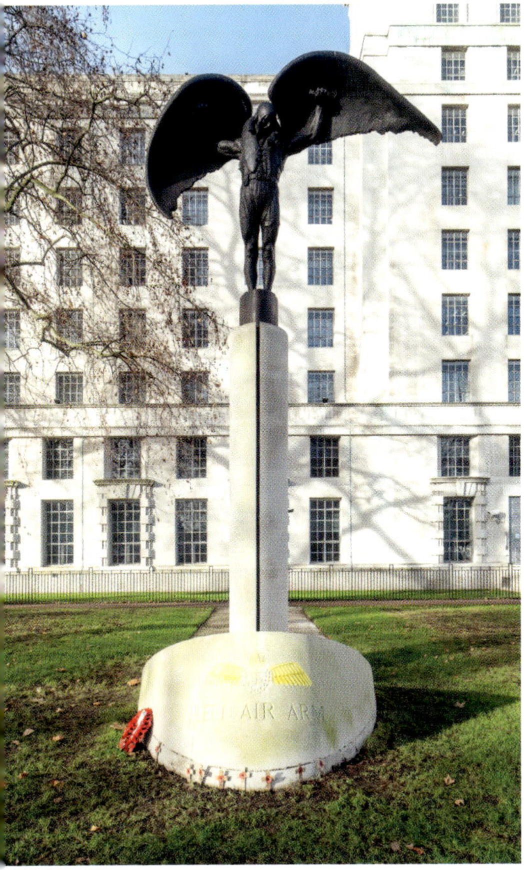

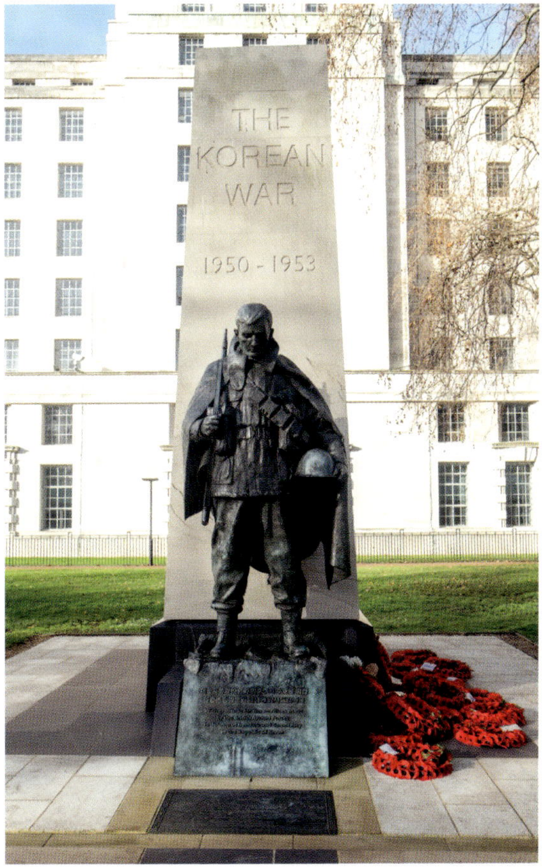

Above left: Fleet Air Arm Memorial with Daedalus by Tim Kempster and James Butler.

Above right: Korean War Memorial by Philip Jackson.

A much-needed four-year refurbishment project led by architects HOK was completed by 2004, including the glazing of the courtyards and with the MoD's 3,000-plus employees all now on one site.

The long south-facing façade provides a perfect backdrop for military memorials. Within Whitehall Gardens, laid out between 1939 and 1959, are memorials for the Chindits, the Iraq and Afghanistan conflicts, Viscount Air Chief Marshal Hugh Trenchard, the Korean War, the Fleet Air Arm (Royal Navy Air Service), 1st Viscount Portal of Hungerford and General Gordon.

Address: Horse Guards Avenue, SW1A 2HB
Built: 1939–51
Listed Status: Grade I
Public Access: No
Tube: Westminster
Website: gov.uk

14. Whitehall Court

Behind Victoria Embankment Gardens appears what resembles a Loire chateau incongruously transplanted to London. Designed and built in two stages by two different architectural practices during the late nineteenth century, various organisations have since occupied it. However, with the two blending into an elaborate but coordinated façade

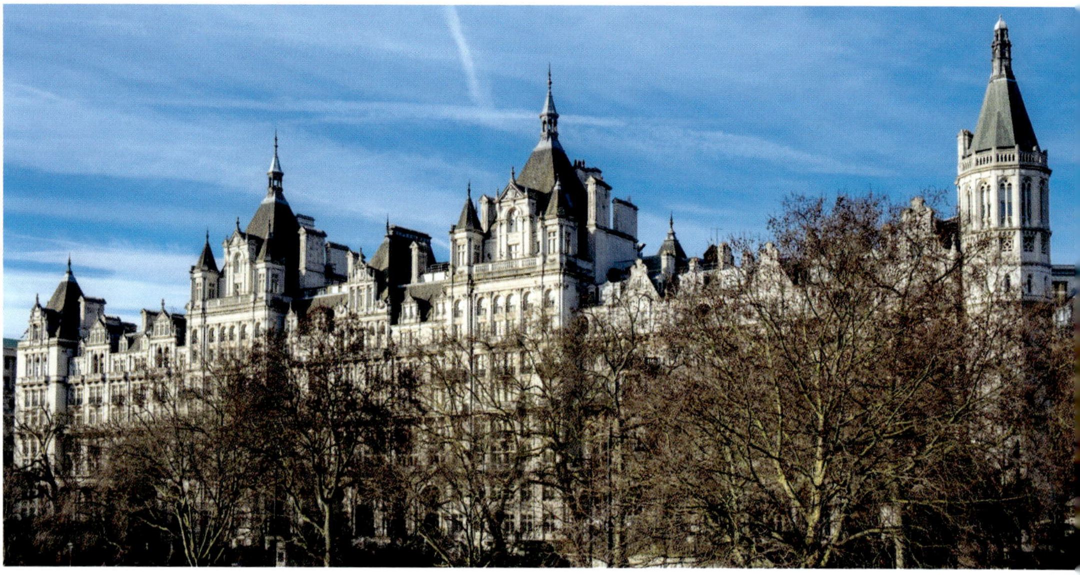

Above and below left: Whitehall Court.

Below right: Nearby the Golden Jubilee bridges link the North and South banks.

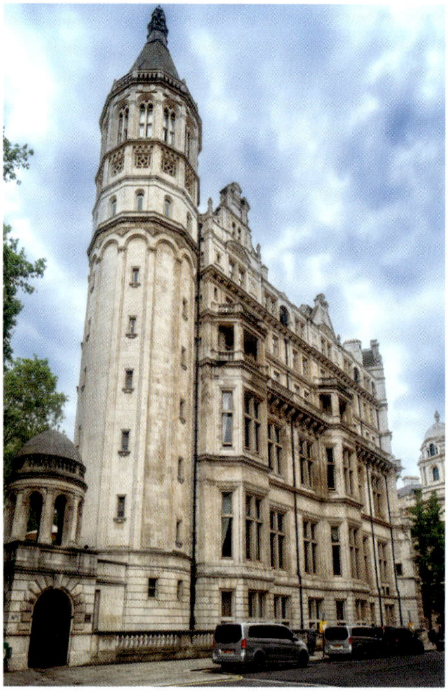

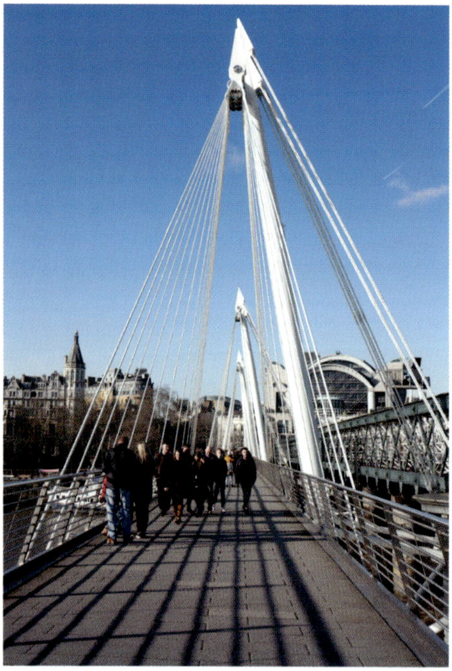

decorated with spirelets, attic windows, gables and, at the eastern flank, a round tower, it appears as one monumental edifice, known as Whitehall Court Nos 1–4.

The southern section was designed by Thomas Archer and Arthur Green for the politician and later fraudster Jabez Balfour (see Entry 22). Opening in 1884, the serviced apartments provided young men about town with a bed and living room plus communal dining facilities. Residents included authors George Bernard Shaw and H. G. Wells and politician William Gladstone.

The northern part was built between 1884 and 1887. Designed by Alfred Waterhouse, architect of the Natural History Museum, No. 1 has been occupied by the National Liberal Club since 1904. Established in 1882, the club was originally for senior Liberals, a political party in power for forty-three of the years between 1852 and 1945. The club offered home-from-home facilities plus opportunities to entertain. Today it is less political than the name implies.

The Royal Horseguards Hotel at No. 2 is the central section. Opened in 1971 having acquired the bedrooms of the club and some of the apartments, it also embraces No. 3, shared with The Farmers Club – No. 3's occupants since 1942, having moved from No. 2. The hotel's restaurant One Twenty-One Two (1212) references New Scotland Yard (see Entry 12) nearby.

The complex has been used for other purposes beyond residential and networking. The MoD, which had established the Secret Intelligence Service (MI6) here in 1911 took possession during the First World War, remaining until 1922. Its first chief, Sir Mansfield Smith-Cumming, commemorated by a blue plaque, lived here during those years.

Address: Whitehall Court, SW1A 2EP
Built: 1882; 1884
Listed Status: Grade II*
Public Access: Yes (Hotel)
Tube/Train: Charing Cross, Embankment
Website: nlc.org.uk

15. Playhouse Theatre

The Playhouse first opened as the Royal Avenue Theatre in 1882. Alongside the Embankment Tube station, its curved Portland stone façade was designed to be visible from the Embankment and, with its pedimented windows at first-floor level, it provides a classical and graceful enhancement to the streetscape.

Like many theatres of the day, it hosted comic operas and burlesques, later presenting dramas including the debut of George Bernard Shaw's *Arms and The Man*. In 1905 it was rebuilt, but during the project, part of the roof of neighbouring Charing Cross railway station (see Entry 17) collapsed onto the theatre, killing six people. The monetary compensation from this tragedy helped fund the current elaborate interior redecoration in French-Venetian style with ornate plasterwork, paintings, curvaceous balconies and walls leading to a dome.

It reopened as the smaller Playhouse Theatre in 1907, and by the 1920s boxes were named after the Prince of Wales and theatrical luminaries, including George Bernard Shaw and Gladys Cooper. In 1951 the BBC acquired it as a radio studio for comedy shows such

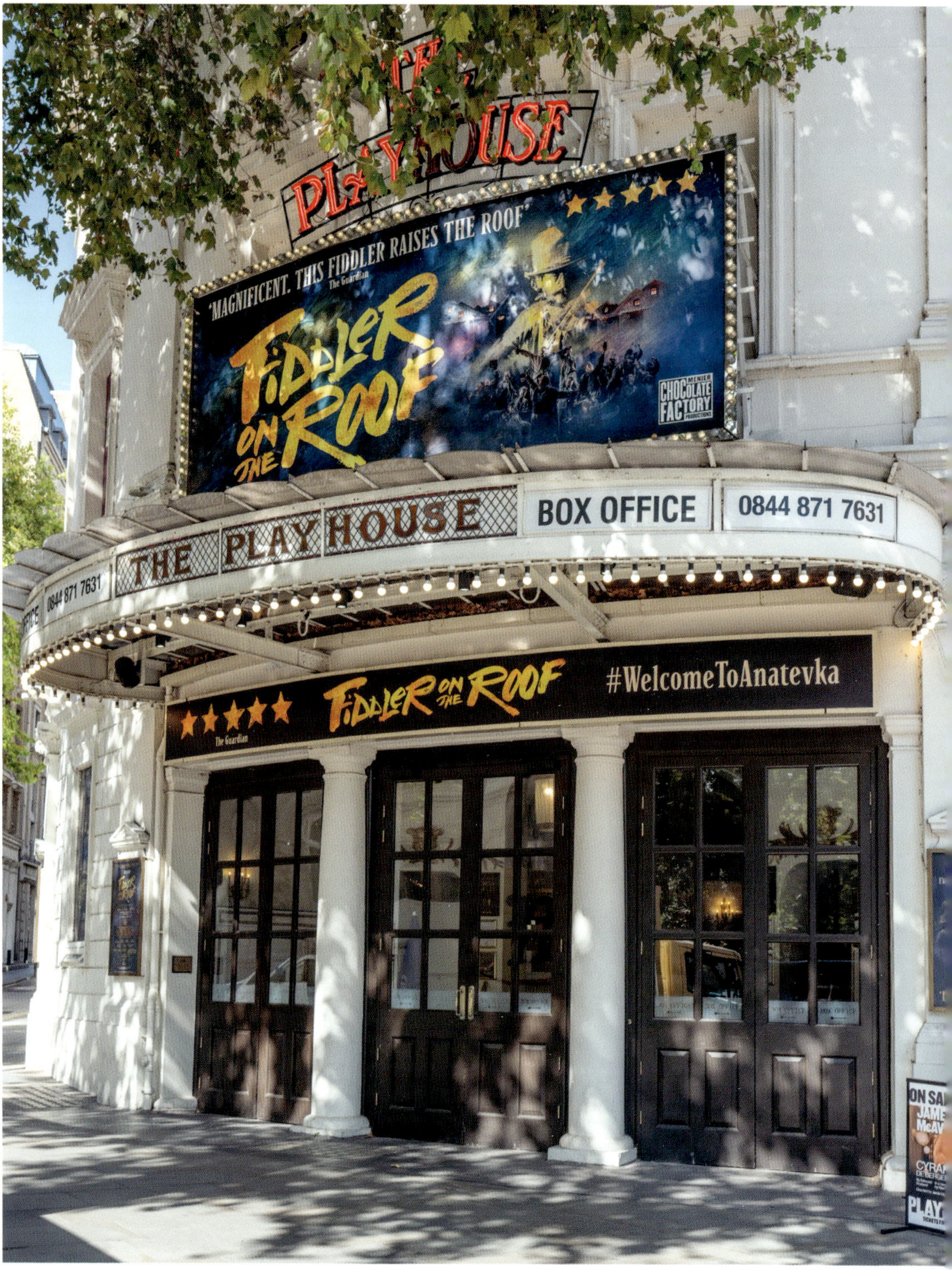

Playhouse Theatre.

as *Hancock's Half Hour* and *The Goon Show* and live band performances, including by The Beatles and The Rolling Stones. After the BBC vacated in 1976, the theatre fell into a state of disrepair until, in 1987, it was restored with a brighter internal colour scheme and reopened. In 1988, it was acquired by politician and author Jeffrey Archer, becoming home in 1991 to the Peter Hall Company. Later bought by comedy farce impresario Ray Cooney, it has been owned by the Ambassador Theatre Group since 2013 and is famous for staging short-run quality drama and musicals.

Address: Northumberland Avenue, WC2N 5DE
Built: 1882; converted 1905
Listed Status: Grade II
Public Access: Yes
Tube/Train: Charing Cross, Embankment
Website: atg.co.uk

16. Cabmen's Shelter

The little green wooden chalet, with its delicate stencilled decoration, outside Embankment Tube station is one of London's thirteen remaining cabmen's shelters. The Cabmen's Shelter Fund, an initiative of Sir George Armstrong, publisher of *The Globe* and *The People*, provided non-alcoholic beverages and wholesome meals swiftly and affordably to cabmen awaiting their next fare, providing an alternative to the temptation of nearby pubs. Cabs at that time were horse-driven carriages and the shelters, positioned on the street, were designed to be no longer than the vehicles stopping there. Inside the cosy cabins were usually wooden built-in benches and panelling. Armstrong provided copies of his own publications as reading material and no card playing or gambling was allowed.

The first shelter opened in 1875 at St John's Wood and by 1889 there were forty. From an estimated peak of sixty-one, they declined rapidly as motor vehicle use grew, but also as London traffic increased they cluttered the roads. Some, repositioned on pavements, continued to provide refreshments and light meals for drivers of black cabs, London's world famous 'cabbies'.

This 1915 Embankment shelter, replacing the 1882 original, was restored in 1991 by the Heritage of London Trust, which has been raising funds since the 1980s to renovate the remaining shelters. From the 2020s, they have also served the public, but for takeaway only. The stencils cleverly spell out 'CSF', the initials of the original scheme.

Another shelter stands on Temple Place, close to Arundel House and Two Temple Place (see Entries 28 and 29), but is not currently offering refreshments.

Address: Embankment Place, WC2N 5AQ
Built: 1915
Listed Status: Grade II
Public Access: Yes
Tube/Train: Embankment

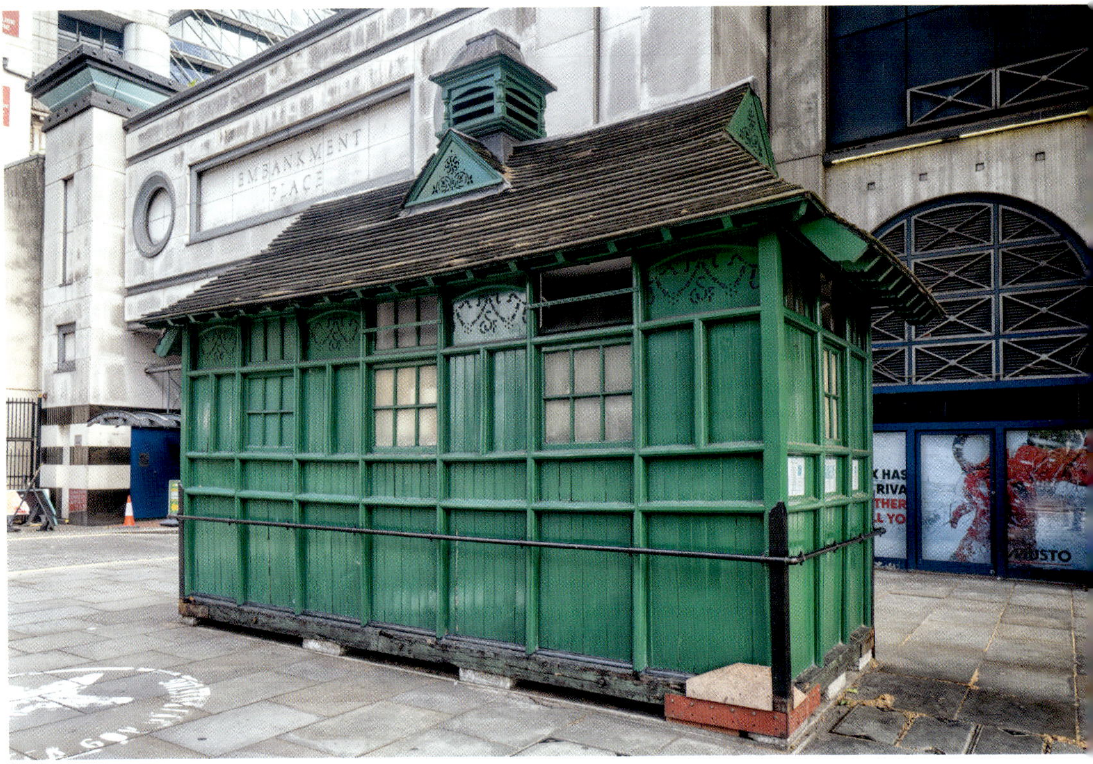

Above and below left: Cabmen's shelter.

Below right: Bazalgette Memorial.

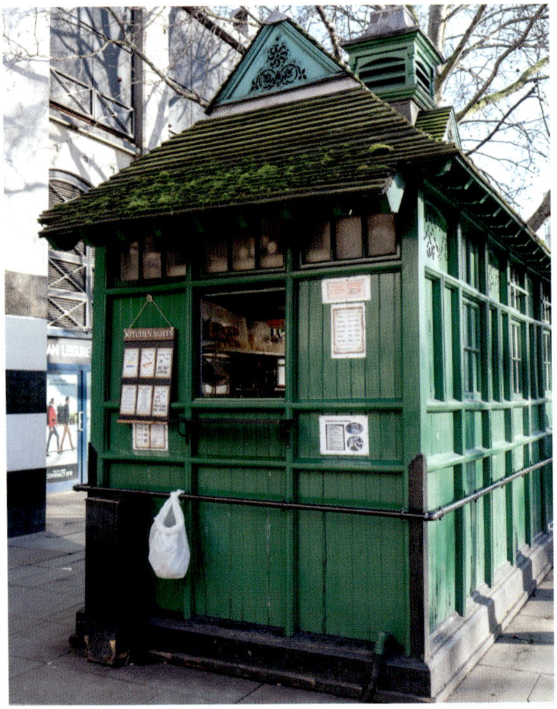

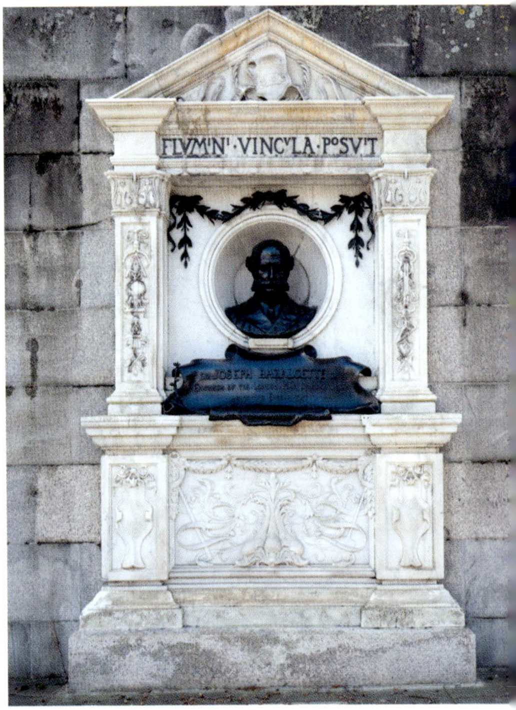

'He put chains on the river', Joseph Bazalgette

London's embankments house a sewer system devised by Joseph Bazalgette for transporting human waste from central London, eradicating regular cholera outbreaks. Prompted by a long hot summer and an unpleasant stench (the Big Stink of 1858), Bazalgette, chief engineer at the Metropolitan Board of Works, devised a reclamation scheme of 37 acres of riverside land, with 20 allocated as public gardens. Over 130 km of sewage piping was then laid underneath. Albert Embankment opened in 1869, followed by Victoria and Chelsea in 1870 and 1874 respectively. The timing coincided with the new underground railways, with the District line extending below the Embankment in 1870. An 1899 memorial to Bazalgette is situated opposite Embankment Tube station.

17. Charing Cross Station

Charing Cross station has a split personality: the Strand has an ornate Victorian frontage, but the riverside fascia is a futuristic postmodern extravaganza from the 1980s.

Designed by Sir John Hawkshaw (see Entry 39), the original station was built on the site of Hungerford Market and opened in 1864, with six platforms covered by a wrought-iron roof 50 metres wide. In 1905 part of the roof collapsed during repairs, resulting in six fatalities and damage to the neighbouring Royal Avenue Theatre (see Entry 15). The ridge and furrow style of the replacement roof was invented by gardener and engineer Joseph Paxton.

The Charing Cross Hotel, designed by E. M. Barry, opened alongside in 1865. Recently renovated it has been rebranded The Clermont. In front of the hotel stands the Eleanor Cross (see Box) from where all distances from London are measured.

During the late 1980s, with space in London at a premium, developers began purchasing air rights above existing properties, with stations a particular target due to their size and central location. The first such station was Charing Cross and between 1985 and 1990 postmodern innovator Terry Farrell designed Embankment Place to straddle the tracks. Looking to some like an ocean liner, to others a giant jukebox, its overall appearance is horizontal, making it seem wider than it is. Incorporated into the new build were offices, retail outlets and high-level pedestrian passageways linking the Embankment and Villiers Street. A nod to the past are the giant initials 'SR' flanking the Southern Railways coat of arms seen from the southern end of the platforms.

Address: Strand, WC2N 5HF
Built: 1864; 1985–1990
Listed Status: Grade II (Hotel)
Public Access: Yes
Tube/Train: Charing Cross, Embankment

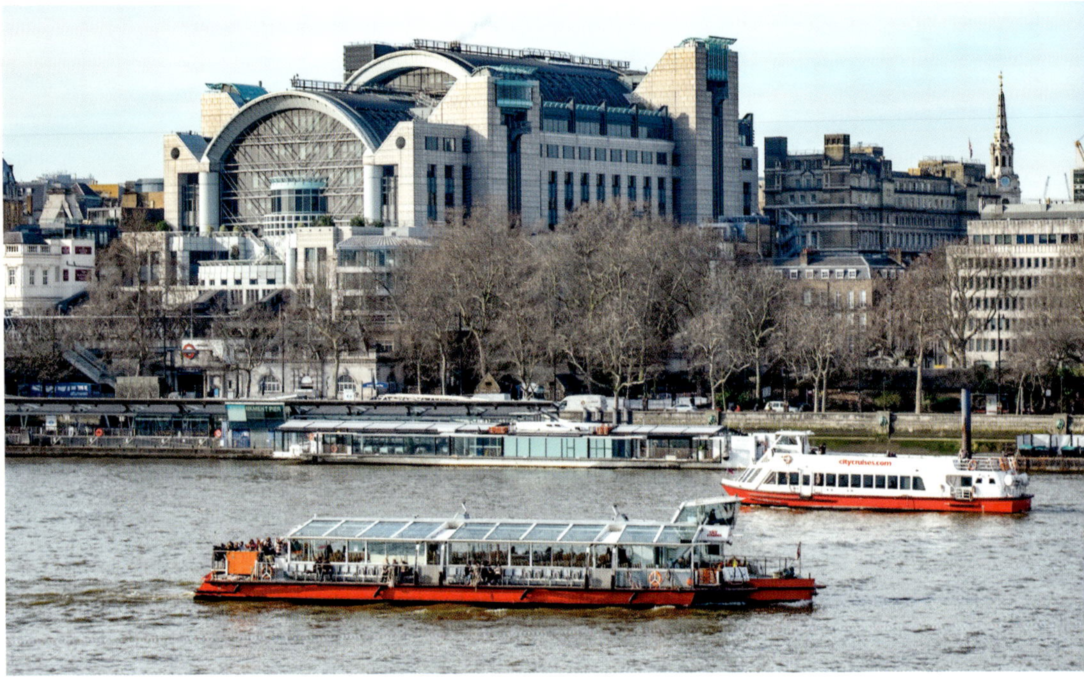

Above and below right: Embankment Place, Charing Cross station.

Below left: Eleanor Cross.

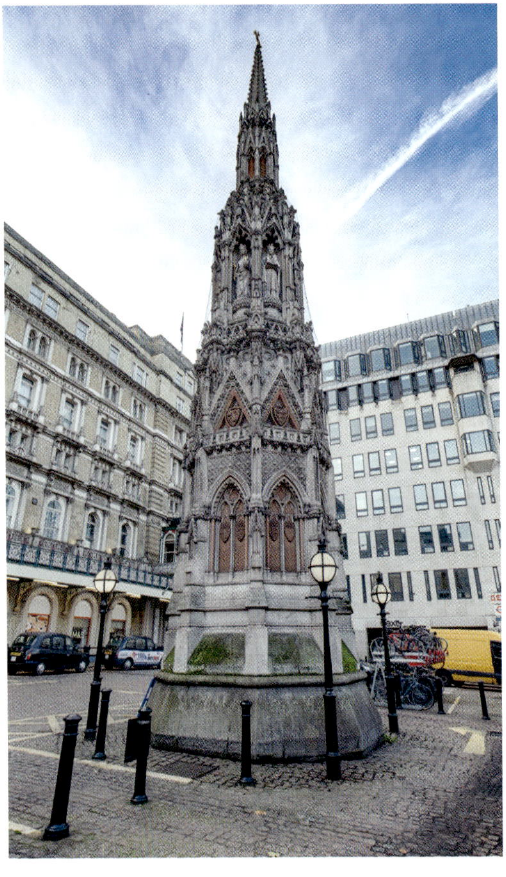

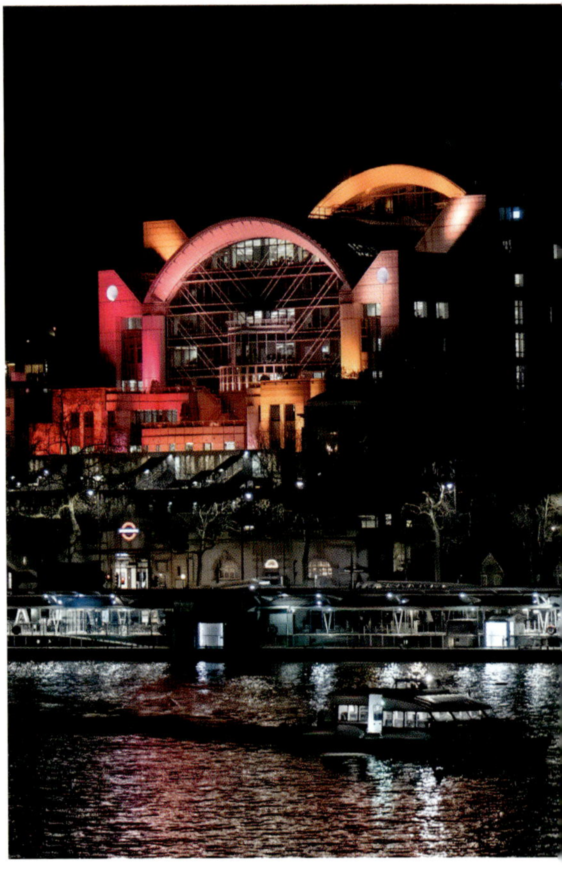

Eleanor Cross

Commissioned by the Charing Cross Hotel Company, designed by station architect E. M. Barry and erected in 1865, decoration includes eight statues of Eleanor of Castille, eight angels and the coats of arms of England, Leon, Castile and Ponthieu. This Grade II* cross replaces the original, sited where the statue of Charles I now stands in Trafalgar Square. Demolished in 1647, it was one of twelve erected along the 1290 funeral route of Queen Eleanor, wife of Edward I, from Lincoln to her burial at Westminster Abbey. Just three survive: at Geddington in Northamptonshire, Hardingstone, Northamptonshire and Waltham Cross in Hertfordshire.

Gordon's Wine Bar

Gordon's Wine Bar on Villiers Street is one of London's most Dickensian drinking places, famous for its ports and sherries. Access from the outside terrace leads to a labyrinth of nooks and crannies where a 1990s renovation has retained 'stabilised dust' for atmosphere. The name dates from 1394 when Arthur 'Staff' Gordon became a 'free vintner', permitted to sell wine without licence. The wine bar opened in 1890 remaining with the Gordon family until Luis Gordon (no relation) took over in 1974.

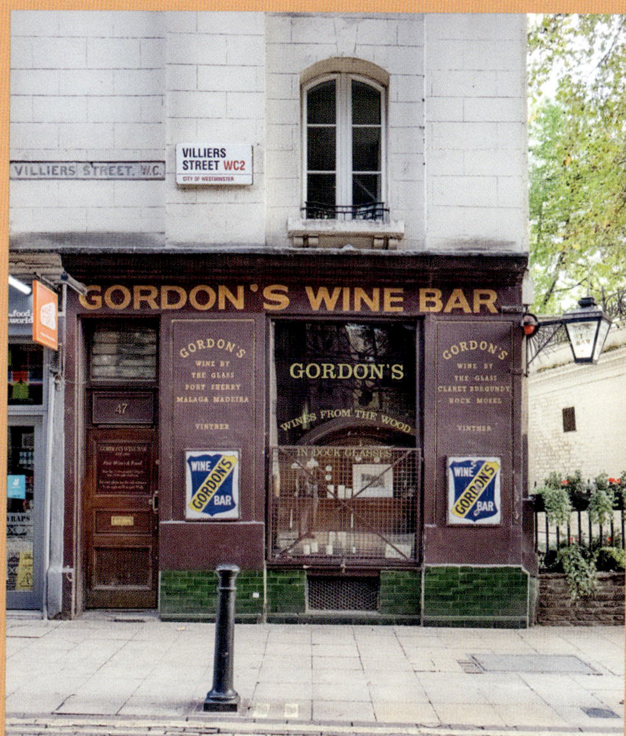

Gordon's Wine Bar.

18. Hungerford House

Currently the ground floor of Hungerford House is a bar and restaurant while the basement hosts a bar and dance venue. These twenty-first-century activities are a far cry from its original function as an electricity sub-station for street lighting built in 1900/01. The design, known as Arts and Crafts Free Style Baroque, includes keystones with light rays in relief, representing energy. Above the entrance sits a maiden with a bobbed haircut seated between a winged lion and a gryphon. The roof is embellished with dormer windows and a cupola. The building was later converted into a library before transformation into the bar.

The name links to Sir Edward Hungerford MP, a seventeenth-century squanderer who established Hungerford Market in 1682. It was never a financial success, despite an 1833 rebuild in Italianate style, and the site was sold to the South Eastern Railway in 1862 for Charing Cross station (see Entry 17). The Hungerford name was retained for the footbridges, first two and later just one, crossing the Thames. They were later rebuilt as two

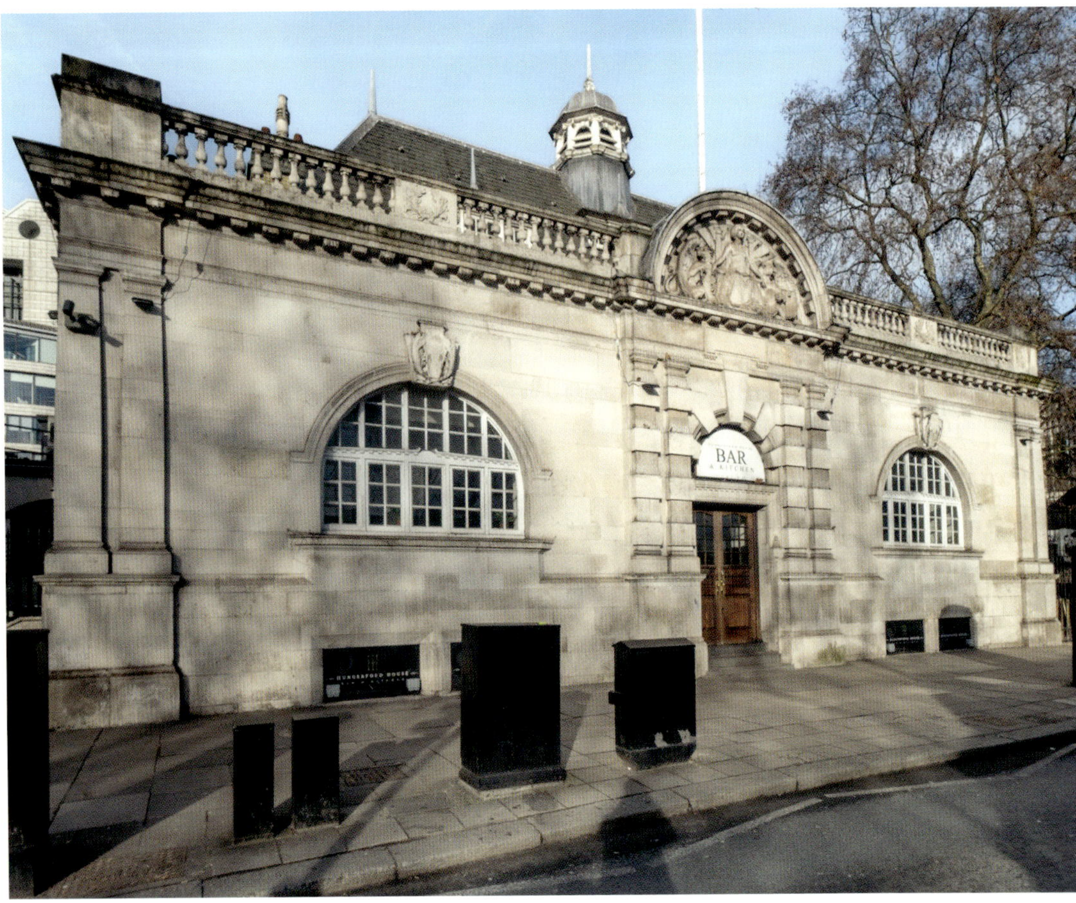

Below and opposite: Hungerford House.

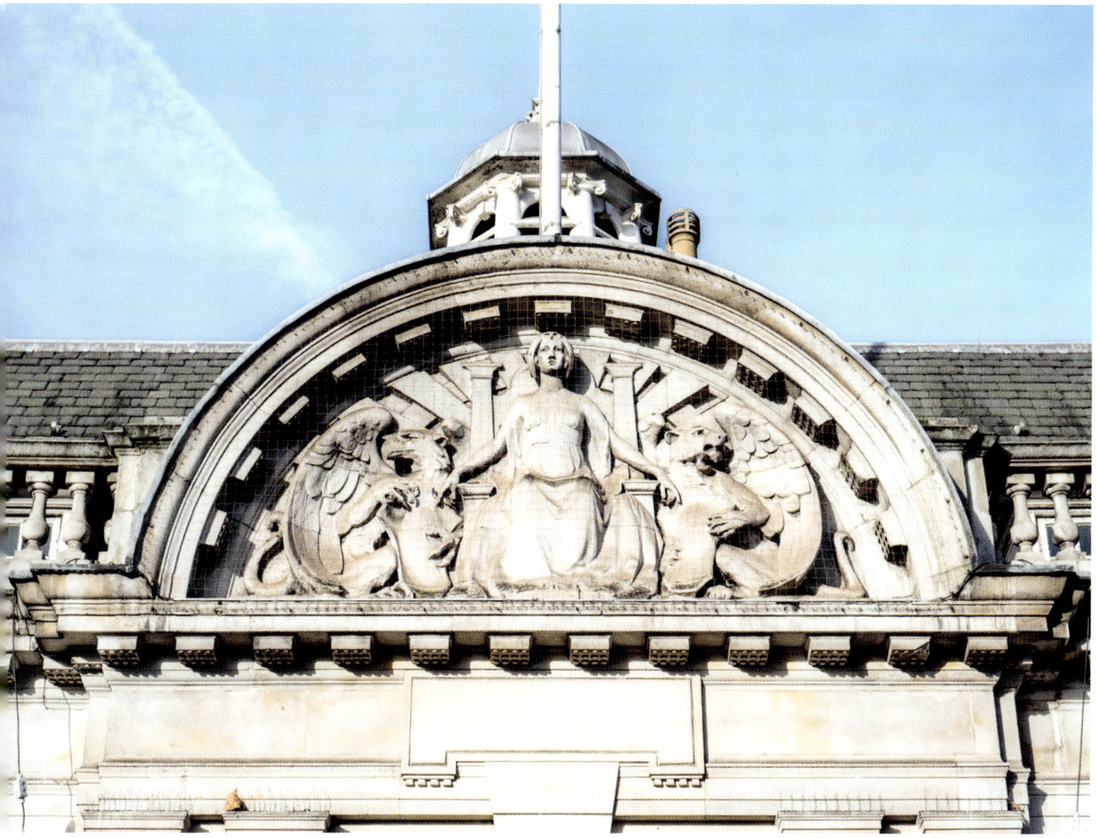

again and renamed the Golden Jubilee Bridges, but are still known as Hungerford Bridge to those who remember the earlier structure.

Address: Victoria Embankment, WC2N 6PA
Built: 1900–01
Listed Status: Grade II
Public Access: Yes
Tube: Embankment
Website: babybullgroup.com

19. York Watergate

This isolated and landlocked stone gateway is one of the few central London reminders of when the Thames was an important highway with high-ranking nobles and clerics owning large homes on the Strand (riverside), each with an impressive gateway for arriving and departing by boat. This site, originally home to the Bishop of Norwich, transferred to the Duke of Suffolk in 1536, becoming the official residence of the Archbishop of York in

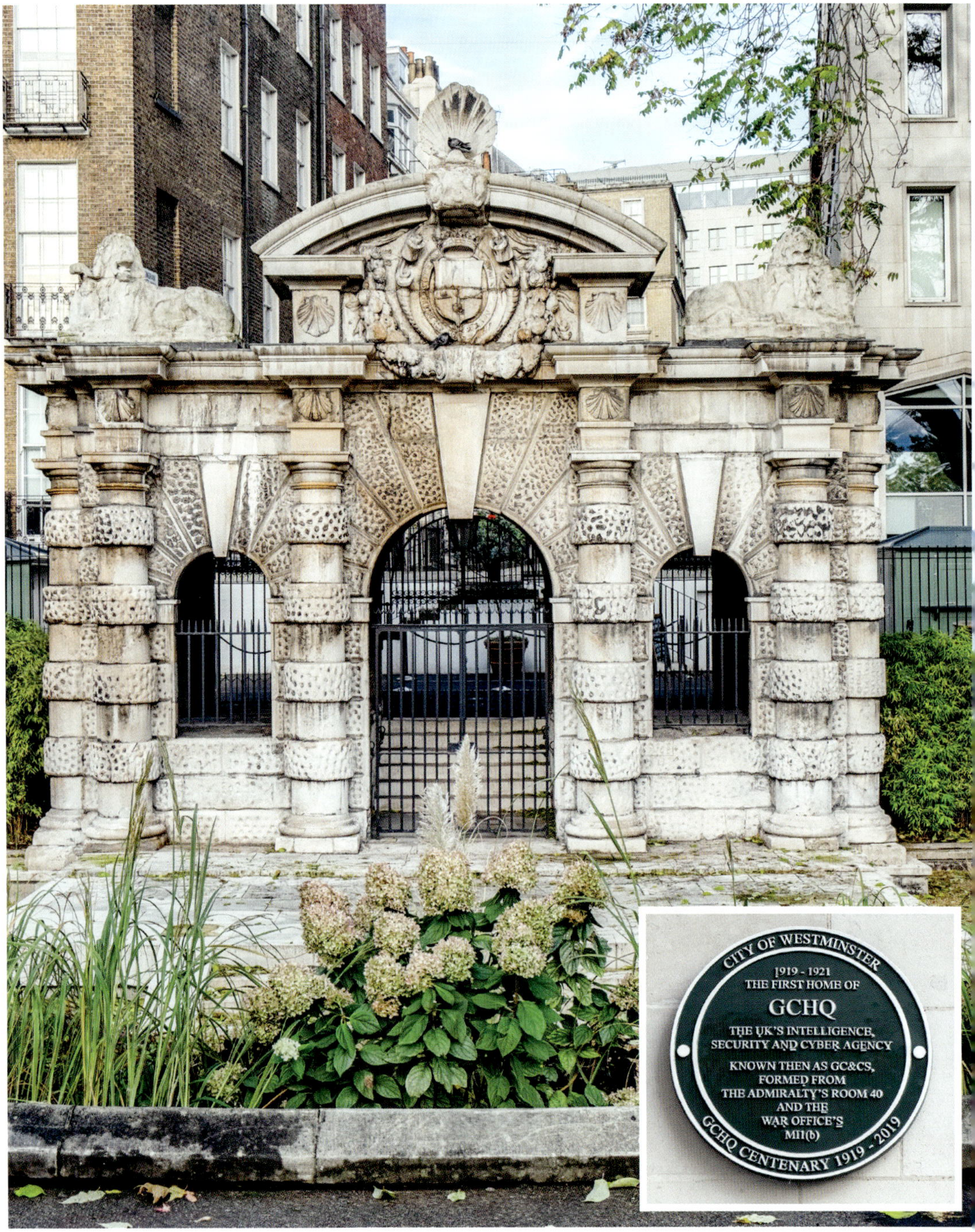

York Watergate. *Inset*: GCHQ centennial plaque incorporating coded message at nearby Watergate House, York Buildings.

1556. It was later gifted by James I to the Duke of Buckingham, who extended the house in the 1620s.

The 2nd Duke, George Villiers, demolished the house, redeveloping the site in 1672 but stipulating he was commemorated, hence Villers, Duke and Buckingham streets, George Court and Of Alley, subsequently renamed York Place. Duke Street has since been subsumed into John Adam Street.

Somehow, the Watergate remained in its initial position, becoming testimony to the breadth of the Thames prior to the construction of the Embankment between 1864 and 1870. Built *c.* 1626 in the style of Inigo Jones, the architect is not known. The coat of arms, seemingly guarded by two lions, is that of the 1st Duke of Buckingham. Above is a giant stone shell with smaller shell motifs below and to both sides. The arch itself has a gateway and two windows with considerable rustication. The north side includes the Buckingham family motto *Fidei Coticula Crux* (the Cross is the Touchstone of Faith) and is topped with a row of four dramatically spiked orbs. The current appearance is the result of LCC restoration in 1898 with regular maintenance since. To date, any proposal to relocate the gate to the riverside has been unsuccessful.

Address: Watergate Walk, WC2N 6DU
Built: *c.* 1626
Listed Status: Grade I
Public Access: Yes
Tube: Embankment

20. RSA

Founded in 1754 by William Shipley as the Society for the Encouragement of Arts, Manufactures and Commerce, it moved here in 1774, received the royal charter in 1847 and adopted the 'Royal' pre-nominal in 1908. Today it is known as the RSA.

RSA House was part of the Adelphi complex (see Entry 21) designed by Scottish neoclassical architect Robert Adam in collaboration with his brothers James, John and William. Adelphi is the Greek word for brothers.

The grand Palladian style entrance on John Adam Street includes four Ionic columns surrounding a Venetian window bordered by a crescent of scallop motifs. Sculptures above the pediment represent arts, manufacture and commerce, a 1994 addition, although to designs by Robert Adam.

Inside, original features include Adam staircases, the Great Room with *The Progress of Human Knowledge* series of paintings by James Barry and fourteen fireplaces, together with works by Gainsborough and Reynolds among others.

The society awarded prizes for challenges, held exhibitions for art and industrial innovations, initiated the Great Exhibition of 1851 and set national exams from 1856.

In 1866 it established the Memorial Tablet scheme. Currently known as the Blue Plaque Scheme and administered by English Heritage, the original plaques were terracotta. The first, unveiled in 1867, commemorated Lord Byron's birthplace, and one on the RSA façade

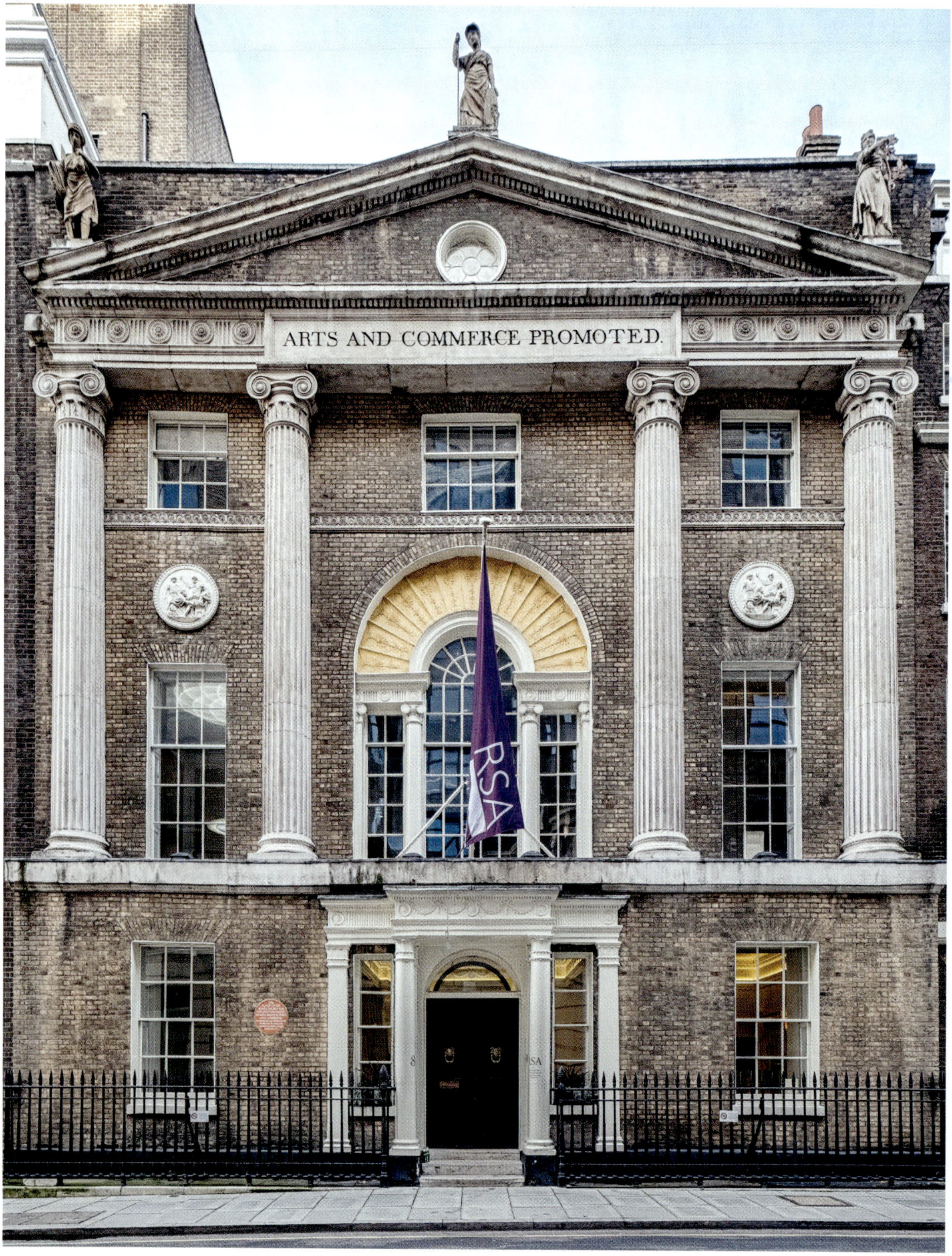

RSA.

commemorates its construction between 1772 and 1774. Plaques recognise sites where people who have made an outstanding impact on society resided or worked. Discovering them unexpectedly is one of the delights of exploring London.

Visible from the Strand at Durham House Street is the RSA rear façade. This view was revealed in the 1920s when offices in front were demolished, and in 1926 this newly seen frontage was redesigned by Sir Aston Webb. The pediment topped with a figure by Walter Gilbert, E. J. Bradford's pilasters and decorative cherubs represent arts, manufacture and commerce. During the 1988–90 conversion new hospitality spaces were created behind the modern arched entry vault.

With 30,000-plus fellows worldwide, it continues to provide a platform for debate and collaboration linked to twenty-first century issues through its Design for Life initiative.

Address: No. 8 John Adam Street, WC2N 6EZ
Built: 1772–74
Listed Status: Grade I
Public Access: By appointment
Tube/Train: Charing Cross, Embankment
Website: thersa.org

21. The Adelphi

A large island block, The Adelphi comprises offices built on the site of the eighteenth-century Adelphi Buildings. These were eleven houses with a vaulted terrace and wharves beneath, built between 1768 and 1772 by the Adam brothers, John, Robert and William – hence John Adam, Robert and Adam streets. A plaque commemorates residents including Richard D'Oyly Carte (see Entry 23) and authors J. M. Barrie, Thomas Hardy and George Bernard Shaw.

Following its demolition in 1936 after an Act of Parliament overturning a 1771 protective covenant, Stanley Hemp of Colcutt & Hemp designed a moderne block of Portland stone around a steel frame. Completed in 1938, eight storeys face John Adam Street with three more to the Embankment side.

The exterior detailing is mostly figurative, with each elevation decorated differently. On Robert Street are insignia of UK cities – Manchester, Leeds and Liverpool – interspersed with reliefs of animals. Turning the corner to the Embankment elevation, known as Adelphi Terrace, a roadway continues beneath an elevated part of the building, passing through an arch surrounded by plump cherubs holding commercial elements such as livestock, fabrics and wheat. Vast allegorical corner sculptures created under the direction of Gilbert Ledward (see Entry 34) represent Dawn, Contemplation, Inspiration and Night. Reliefs of zodiac signs lead to the main doorway where the double-height entrance is framed with two stone murals by interwar sculptor Newbury Abbott Trent showcasing British industry. Created in 1938, one represents workmen, sleeves rolled up and wearing hobnailed boots, while the other depicts shipbuilding, with bare-chested men hauling ropes amid mooring rings and lifebelts. Large gold lettering above the entrance was designed by George Manswell and below the parapet are small reliefs of different flowers.

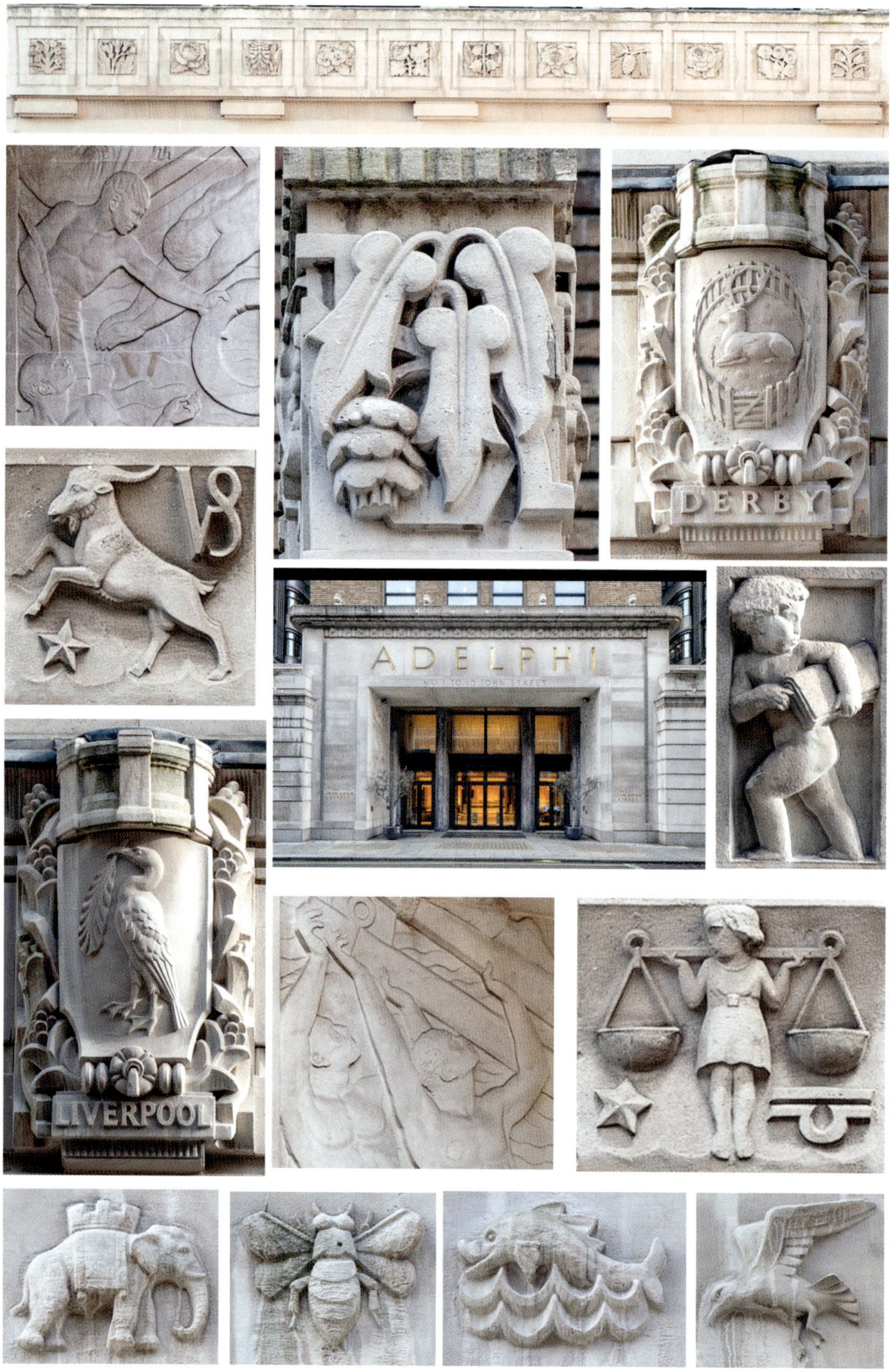

The Adelphi.

The building embraced not only modern architecture but modern society, as it incorporated a car park. In 1993 an additional two storeys were added.

Inside, original art deco marble flooring, etched glass panels and brass handrails survive, with the building currently home to various businesses including *The Economist* and *Vogue* magazines.

Address: Nos 1–11 John Adam Street, WC2N 6HT
Built: 1936–38
Listed Status: Grade II
Public Access: No
Tube/Train: Charing Cross, Embankment
Website: adelphibuilding.com

22. Shell Mex House

The newly configured courtyard at No. 80 Strand is a recent redevelopment by architect Duncan Mitchell, remodelling an early 1930s Portland stone art deco office block.

The project seamlessly connected the colonnaded Strand fascia via the courtyard to a double-height interior atrium which references the original 1930s design, including polished plaster panelling, decorative metalwork and fluted glass and bronze wall and ceiling lighting.

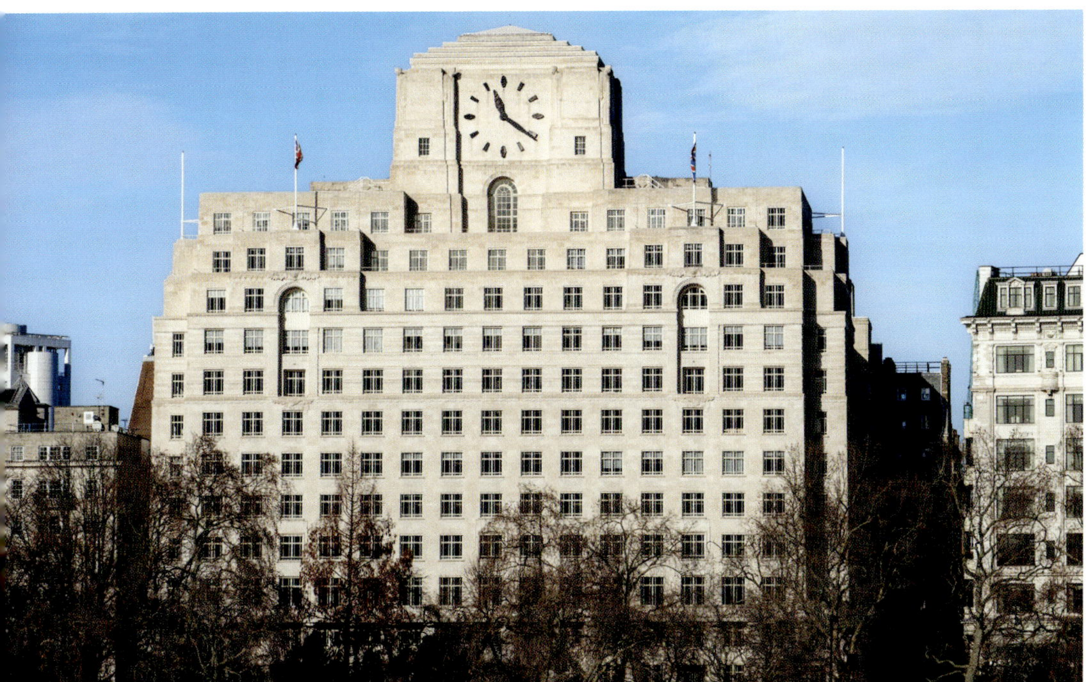

Shell Mex House (Big Benzene).

There is a second entrance at the south side from Embankment Gardens where the façade is stepped back at the upper levels, showcasing the range of heights from eleven to fifteen storeys. Exterior decoration includes four marble sculptures by W. C. H. King to an Egyptian design known as hieratic, linked to priestly worship, with the wide tower adorned with the UK's largest clock face, 7.62 metres in diameter, making this one of central London's most recognisable landmarks.

Once known as Big Benzene, it was built in 1930/31 for Shell Mex and British Petroleum (BP) as their joint enterprise HQ. Opened in 1933 to designs by Messrs Joseph, it incorporated the Strand fascia from the previous building on the site, Hotel Cecil, then Europe's largest hotel.

Building started in 1890, but proprietor Jabez Balfour MP (see Entry 14) had used funds from his Liberator Building Society and, following its 1892 collapse and his subsequent conviction, the hotel with its 800-plus rooms and 600-cover dining room was completed by new owners in 1896. The hotel was named after Robert Cecil, Secretary of State to Elizabeth I, who lived in Salisbury House, previously on this site.

In 1918 it was requisitioned as the newly formed Royal Air Force HQ (see Entry 34). In 1919 the hotel reverted to hospitality before being largely demolished, leaving the Strand frontage intact. At the outbreak of the Second World War the building was temporarily taken over, appropriately, by the Petroleum Board to administer and regulate fuel supplies and usage.

Shell, sole tenants since 1976, moved out in 2020, following the end of the joint venture, the building having been acquired by the German Conle family in 2013.

Address: No. 80 Strand, WC2R 0BP
Built: 1932
Listed Status: Grade II
Public Access: No
Tube/Train: Charing Cross

23. Savoy Hotel

The south elevation of the Savoy Hotel as seen from the Victoria Embankment Gardens gives little indication of the luxury within. However, accessing the hotel from the Strand visitors pass decorative information boards outlining the history of Count Peter of Savoy (see Entry 24), who has greeted everyone from the entrance canopy since 1929, resplendent in his armour, shield and pennant, a gleaming 1904 statue sculpted by Frank Lynn Jenkins.

When Richard D'Oyly Carte was building a theatre for his productions of Gilbert & Sullivan operas on the site of Savoy Palace, Savoy was an obvious choice of name. Designed by eminent theatre architect C. J. Phipps, the theatre opened in 1881. State-of-the-art facilities included electricity and innovations included numbered seats, free programmes, 'proper' whiskey and a no-tipping cloakroom. It was refurbished in 1929 by Basil Ionides in art deco style with pastel zinnia upholstery. Following a disastrous 1990 fire, the original Ionides design was restored.

The early theatre's rapid success enabled D'Oyly Carte to invest the profits into building a hotel alongside. The Savoy Hotel, designed by T. E. Collcutt, opened in 1889

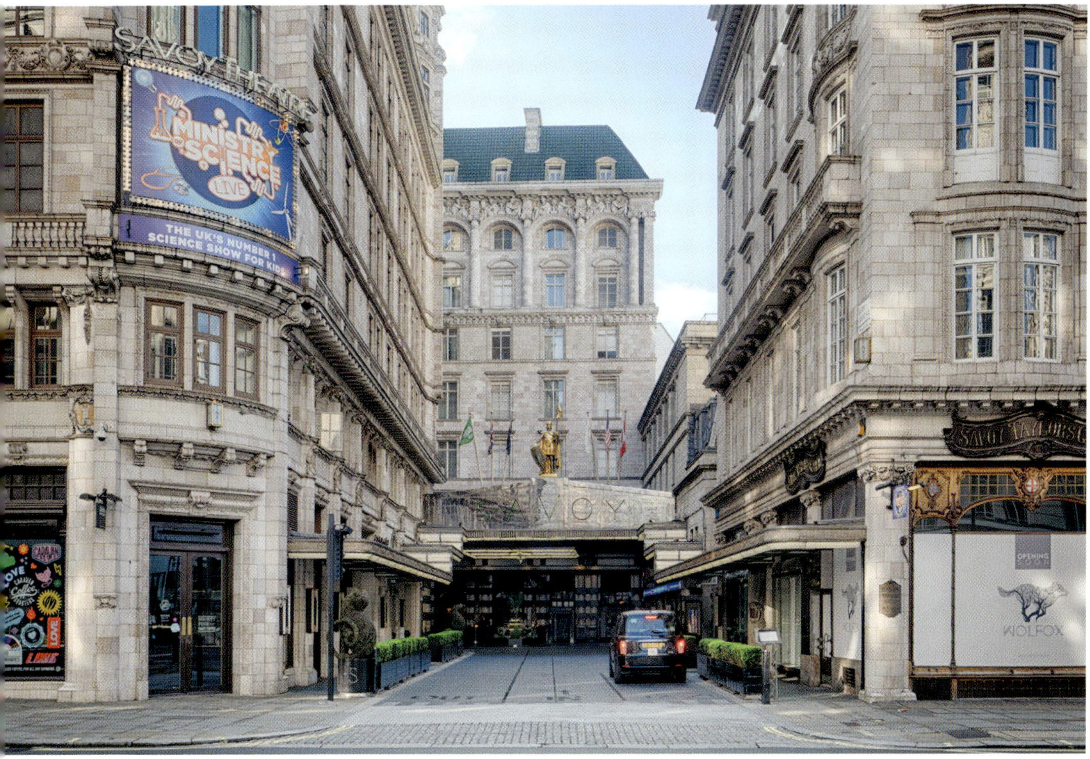

Above: Savoy Hotel.

Below left: Caspar the Cat.

Below right: Memorial sundial to the D'Oyly Carte family celebrating the Savoy centenary, outside south entrance.

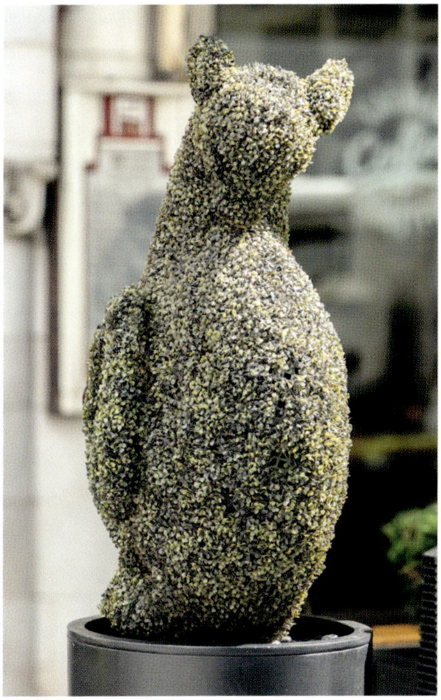

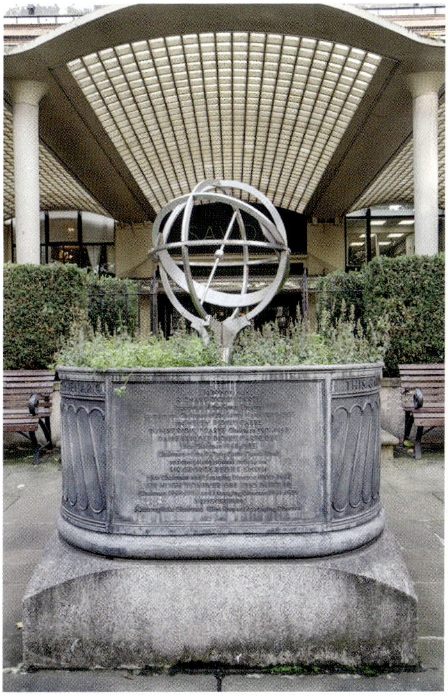

with the first blocks to the south, and the Strand block opening in 1904. It was a byword for luxury, with César Ritz the first manager and Auguste Escoffier his head chef. Despite both being sacked in 1897 for misappropriation of food and wine, the Savoy maintained a high reputation and over the decades became the hotel of choice for celebrities including Oscar Wilde, Charlie Chaplin and Bob Dylan. It was here that opera singer Dame Nellie Melba had two dishes devised for her delicate diet, Melba Toast and Peach Melba, while Eggs Arnold Bennett, a smoked haddock omelette, was invented for the author.

The road entrance serving both hotel and theatre is the only London thoroughfare permitting motor vehicles to drive on the right-hand side, allowing theatregoers to alight directly by the theatre entrance. Two large cats made of artificial hedge represent Caspar, the wooden cat carved by Ionides and added to a hotel dining table of thirteen guests to make fourteen, preventing potential ill luck linked to the number thirteen. The story dates to 1898 when Woolf Joel, a wealthy diamond magnate, hosted a dinner party at the Savoy for thirteen people only to be murdered in South Africa a few weeks later.

There have been several hotel proprietors and regular upgrades, with current owners, Fairmont, initiating a three-year refurbishment project in 2007, retrospectively part-funded by an auction in 2012 of 3,000 hotel artefacts from ashtrays to chandeliers.

Address: Strand, WC2R 0EZ
Built: 1889
Listed Status: Grade II
Public Access: Yes
Tube/Train: Charing Cross
Website: thesavoylondon.com

24. The King's Chapel of the Savoy

The name Savoy links back to 1246 when land was granted to Count Peter of Savoy (see Entry 23), uncle of Eleanor of Provence, wife of Henry III. Although he did not own it for long, he built a palace and his name remained. The palace was destroyed during the Peasants' Revolt of 1381 and rebuilt but was cleared by Henry VII in 1505 for an extensive complex comprising a hospital tending 100 'pour and nedie' men, three chapels dedicated to St Catherine, Our Lady and St John the Baptist, and a dormitory over 60 metres long. All that survives is a stone chapel with a bell turret and graveyard, now a secluded oasis for local workers and visitors.

The chapel was a place of worship between the 1490s and 1512, but, following the neighbourhood's rapid population growth, by 1598 social commentator John Stow noted many 'vagabonds, loiterers and strumpets'. The hospital became used by the military and the foundation dissolved in 1702. The buildings were demolished in the 1720s except for St John's Chapel, now officially the King's Chapel of the Savoy. After repairs by Robert Smirke (see Entry 46) between 1820 and 1821, further restoration during the 1880s by Robert's brother Sydney followed fires in 1843 and 1864. The stunning ceiling by Thomas Willement from the original Tudor design is studded with royal coats of arms, quatrefoils and the Lancastrian white rose. The distinctive deep cobalt blue and the golden Christian motifs above the chancel were added during restoration in 1999. Angels adorn the frieze immediately below the ceiling and there are multiple stained-glass windows, including

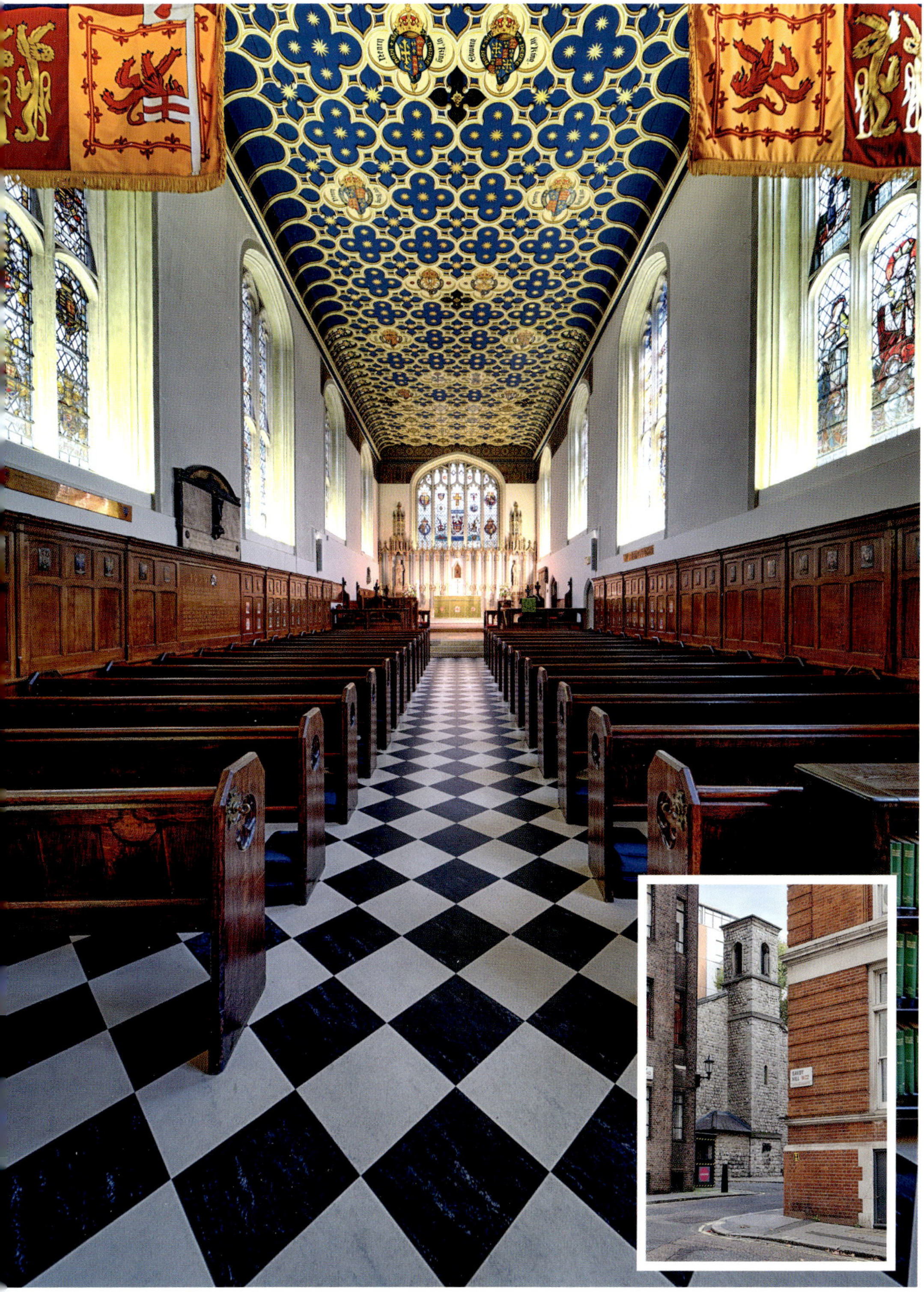

The King's Chapel of the Savoy.

those honouring D'Oyly Carte (see Entry 23) family members, the Silver Jubilee of George V and the Diamond Jubilee of Queen Elizabeth II, incorporating her signature, a corgi dog, a horse and typefaces from 1952 and 2012.

The chapel was rededicated as the Royal Victorian Order (RVO) Chapel in 1937 by King George VI. The RVO, a personal gift bestowed by the monarch, was established in 1896 by Queen Victoria to honour service to the sovereign. RVO holders past and present are represented by flags and name plaques.

Address: Savoy Hill, WC2R 0DA
Built: 1490/1512
Listed Status: Grade II*
Public Access: Yes
Tube: Temple

25. Institution of Engineering and Technology

Above the main entrance at No. 2 Savoy Place is the coat of arms of the Institution of Engineering and Technology (IET). This is its HQ, archives and library but also a popular event space, its terrace offering magnificent views across the river. Established in 1871 as

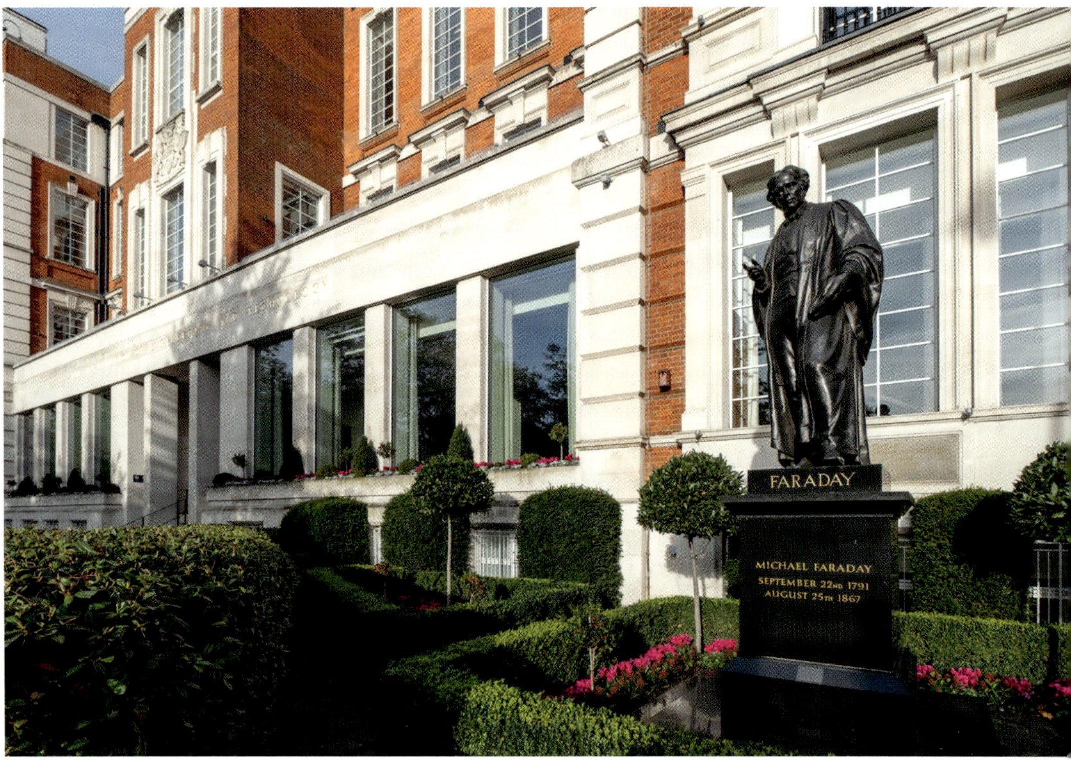

Institution of Engineering and Technology.

the Society of Telegraph Engineers, in 1889 it became the Institution of Electrical Engineers (IEE) and moved here in 1909 during an expansion of membership from *c.* 2,000 in 1895 to over 7,000 by 1914.

The building looked very different then, having been built in 1889 as the Medical Examination School for the Royal College of Physicians and Royal College of Surgeons (RCS). Designed by Stephen Salter, architect to the RCS, and H. Percy Adams, his colleague who later worked with Charles Holden, famous for several Tube stations, it had a red-brick and Portland stone frontage. The two ends protruded towards the Thames, with a shallower central section housing the entrance, but by the mid-twentieth century the IEE required additional space. Between 1958 and 1960 Adams, Holden & Pearson refaced the south side, added a new floor with a larger lecture theatre and incorporated more galleries, a new meeting room and state-of-the-art audio-visual facilities. In 2006 the IEE became the IET.

Commemorated by a large tablet on the west wing are nine years' residency of the BBC on IEE premises. Formed in 1923, the newly established BBC leased space here to broadcast live radio drama and weather forecasts. It remained until 1932, having expanded into the adjacent Savoy Mansions in 1925.

Outside stands a statue, commissioned in the 1980s, of scientist Michael Faraday, a pioneer of electrical engineering and Scientific Advisor to Trinity House (see Entry 49).

It is a replica of his 1876 statue at the Royal Institution, where he is depicted lecturing at No. 9 Millbank (see Entry 6).

Address: No. 2 Savoy Place, WC2R 0BL
Built: 1889; 1958–60
Public Access: No
Tube: Temple
Website: savoyplace.theiet.org

26. Brettenham House

Walking over Waterloo Bridge towards the Strand, to the right Somerset House (see Entry 27) dominates the view despite the bulk of a vast art deco office block to the left that is Brettenham House.

Designed by father and son William and Edward Hunt and completed in 1932, the twelve-storey office block is clad in Portland stone. The top levels are stepped back and retail spaces incorporated at ground level.

Exterior decoration is minimal, with the name of the building and the numbers '5' and '6' in metallic relief on the bridge-approach door. Colour is only found enhancing the coats of arms for the City of Westminster and the Duchy of Lancaster, the latter the site's freeholder. The designs are two portcullises with Tudor roses and three golden lions bordered by two white feathers respectively.

The Duchy, headquartered at No. 1 Lancaster Place at the southern end but named separately, is a private estate owned by the King, who is also Duke of Lancaster. In addition to 44,748 acres of rural estate, the Duchy owns urban land of which the Savoy estate, including the King's Chapel of the Savoy (see Entry 24), is the largest part. Coastline, mineral deposits

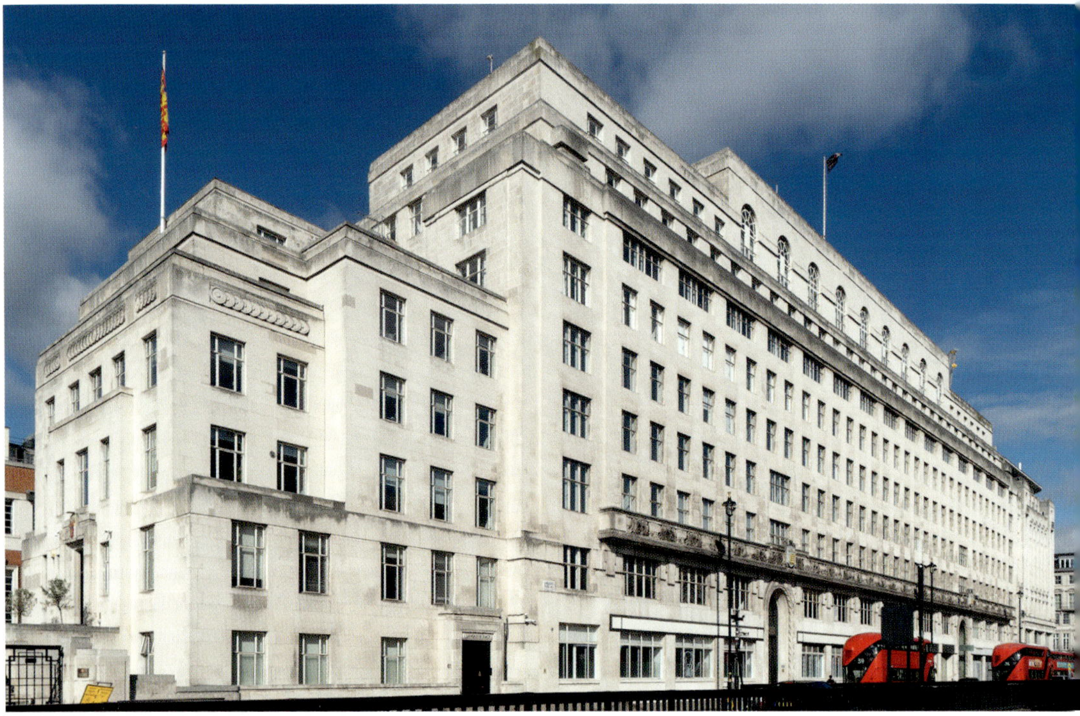

Above and below: Brettenham House.

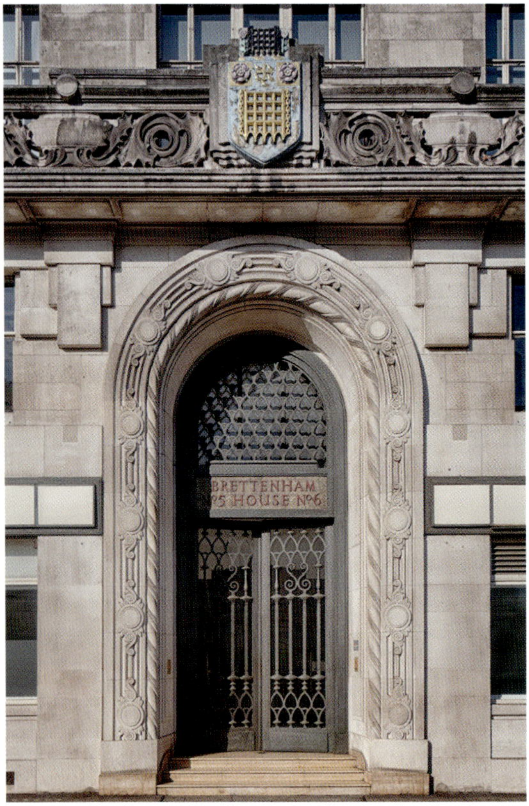

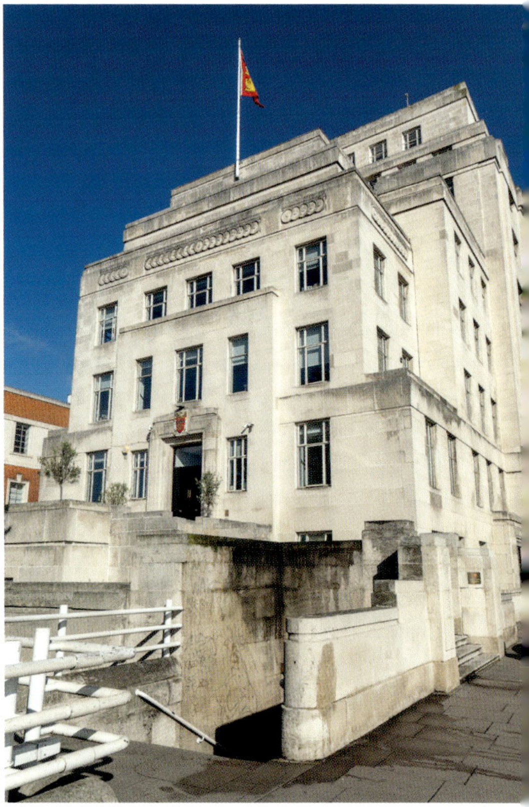

and castles across England and Wales complete the Duchy's holdings. A boundary marker for the Duchy is found at the foot of the west steps from the Embankment to Waterloo Bridge.

Brettenham House remained largely unaltered until a recent lengthy process of internal refurbishment.

Address: Nos 1–19 Lancaster Place, London, WC2 7EN
Built: 1932
Public Access: No
Tube: Temple
Website: brettenhamhouse.com

27. Somerset House

With magnificent frontages on both the Strand and Victoria Embankment, Somerset House is a palatial building with a long and varied history beginning with a Tudor palace built by Edward Seymour, Duke of Somerset and Protector during the reign of Edward VI, the son of his sister Jane and Henry VIII. For centuries Somerset House was used as accommodation for royal guests, courtiers and dowager queens.

Having been ravaged during Oliver Cromwell's Republic with valuable art and furnishings sold off, by the late 1700s the palace was both in disrepair and surplus to requirements. George III brokered a deal exchanging Buckingham House (now Palace) for the dilapidated Somerset House and the site was rebuilt between 1776 and 1801 for various government departments and learned societies. Surrounding a central courtyard and cleverly designed by William Chambers to resemble a series of town houses, three storeys of offices are visible and a further three hidden – one at roof level and two in the basement. Each tenant was allocated a six-storey section, with carved stone naval motifs indicating the Navy Board offices and Father Thames seen below a relief of George III. Other early tenants included Stamp Duty and Victualling offices and the Royal Academy of Arts. Following Chambers' death in 1776, James Pennethorne added a western wing.

East of the riverside terrace is an entry to King's College, established in 1829. Designed by Robert Smirke and completed in 1831, its founders were granted use of surplus land on condition that the architecture blended with Chambers' original plans.

Below, a giant shallow arch built for the Navy Board's gilded barge to enter and now marooned on the Embankment is another reminder of the original breadth of the Thames (see Entries 19, 50).

On the Strand elevation eight British rivers are represented by keystones, with a series of male faces showcasing an astonishing array of beards and whiskers. By the early twentieth century Somerset House was used solely by the Civil Service, including the Inland Revenue and Births, Deaths and Marriages registry and later the grand courtyard was employee parking. A 1977 campaign by the *Evening Standard* newspaper led to a radical transformation. Government officials departed and by 2000 the car park was filled with dancing fountains, while tenants included the Courtauld art collection (in situ since 1932) and the Gilbert Collection (now at the V&A Museum) alongside eateries and exhibition spaces. The restored basements and staircases, including the Nelson Stair leading to the

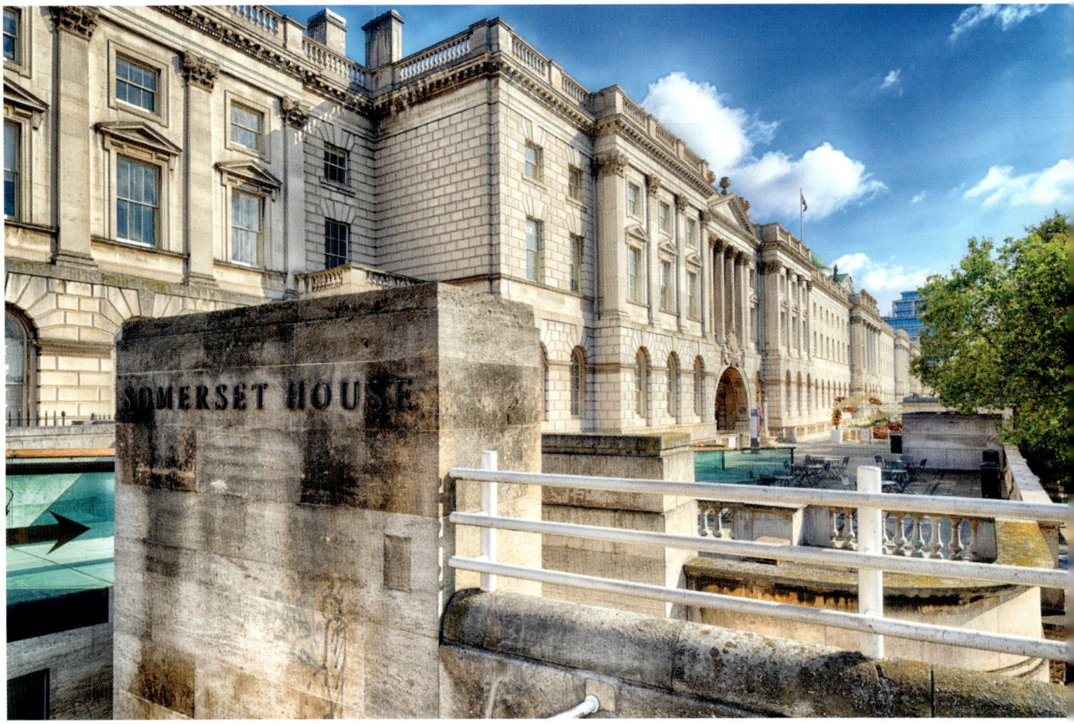

Above, below left and below right: Somerset House.

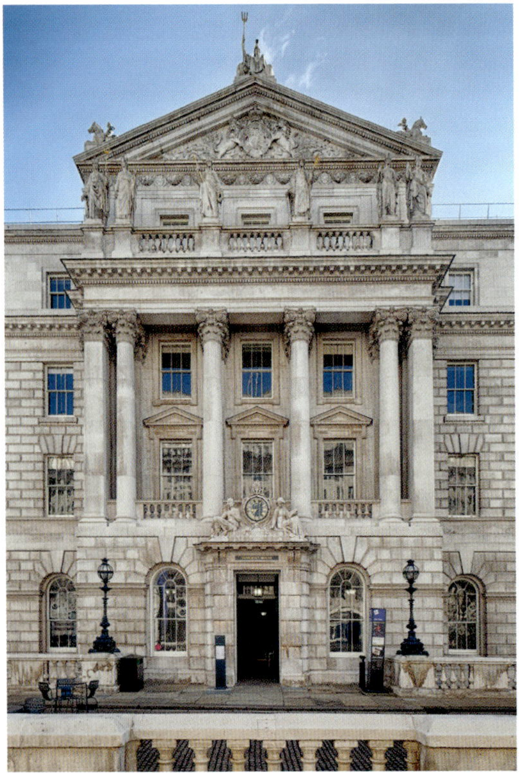

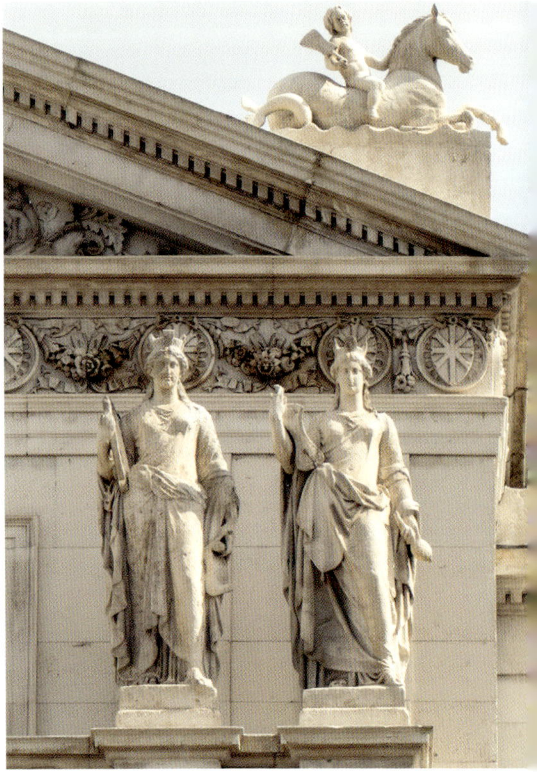

Navy Office Boardroom, provide public access to all levels and the courtyard hosts seasonal outdoor events.

Address: Strand, London, WC2R 1LA
Built: 1776–1801
Listed Status: Grade I
Public Access: Yes
Tube: Temple
Website: somersethouse.org.uk

28. Arundel House

The ornate red-brick building on the corner of Arundel Street and Temple Place resembles an aristocratic Tudor town house but was actually built in 1884 for Henry Fitzalan-Howard, the 15th Duke of Norfolk.

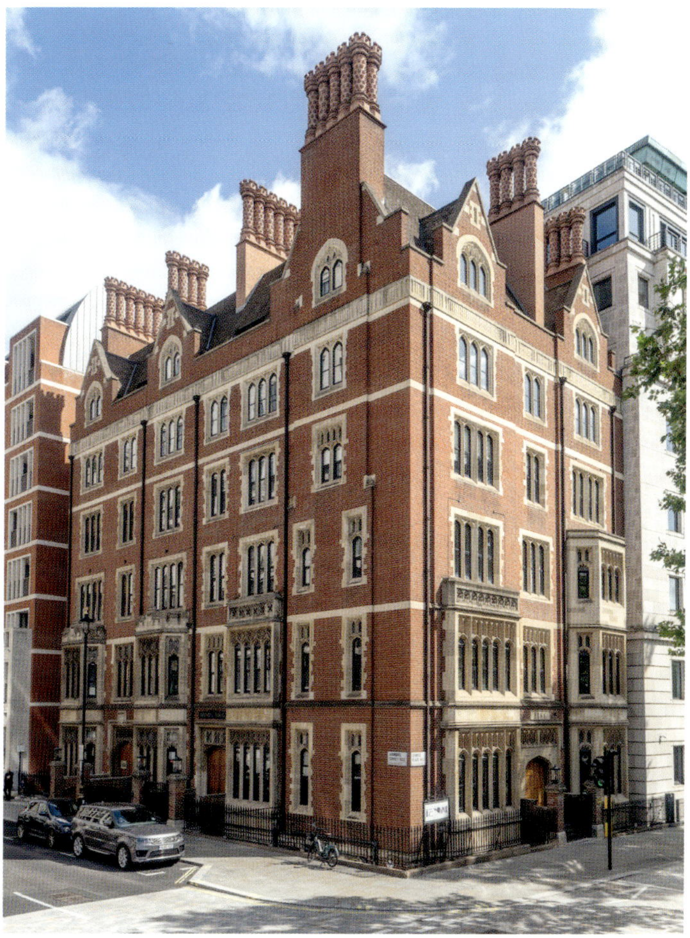

Arundel House.

Arundel House and Street are both named after the Howard family's original London town house and following demolition in 1678, the site became a grid of streets named Howard, Norfolk and Surrey. Howard is the surname for the Duchy of Norfolk, the UK's most senior Roman Catholic family. Each Duke of Norfolk has the role of Earl Marshal, an important ceremonial position created in 1672 with responsibility for state occasions including coronations, jubilees and the State Opening of Parliament. The Howards also own an ancestral castle in Arundel, West Sussex.

Referencing the original Arundel House, the Howard family's land agent and architect John Dunn used red brick and terracotta in Tudorbethan style, a combination of Tudor and Elizabethan sixteenth-century design. The windows are surrounded by carved stonework and crenelated chimneys stand on a gabled rooftop.

Entrances at Nos 13–15 Arundel Street were used as an address for the UK HQ for Marvel Comics between the late 1980s and 1995.

Since 1997 Arundel House, branded as Six Temple Place, has been the headquarters for the International Institute for Strategic Studies (IISS), a respected think tank for global security, political risk and military conflict, established in 1958. The IISS commissioned a dramatic remodelling incorporating an additional floor just below the rooftop, completed in 2001.

Address: Six Temple Place, WC2R 2PG
Built: 1884
Public Access: No
Tube: Temple
Website: iiss.org

29. Two Temple Place

Set back from the eastern end of Victoria Embankment Gardens is a building with an array of embellishments, each of which seem to bear no relationship to each other: a hanging sign depicting a bulldog, a glistening golden ship weathervane and four green oxidised bronze cherubs – two listening and speaking on a telephone, the others holding a light bulb and electric coil. Carved heads with dramatic expressions by Nathaniel Hitch (see Entry 35) peek out below the crenelated rooftop.

This eclectic exterior of Portland stone in Tudorbethan style, not unlike that of Arundel House (see Entry 28), belongs to Two Temple Place, built in 1895 for William Waldorf Astor, later Viscount, as his business HQ.

In 1890, Astor, an American, inherited great wealth from his father John Astor, the railroads magnate. He then made his own fortune opening the Waldorf Hotel but relocated to the UK where he thought his finances and family would be safer. He commissioned John Loughborough Pearson, an architect renown for elaborate designs, to ensure his HQ was secure and could store and showcase his valuable art collection and library. His obsession with security meant that Pearson's design incorporated a complex web of locks, secret doors and drawers.

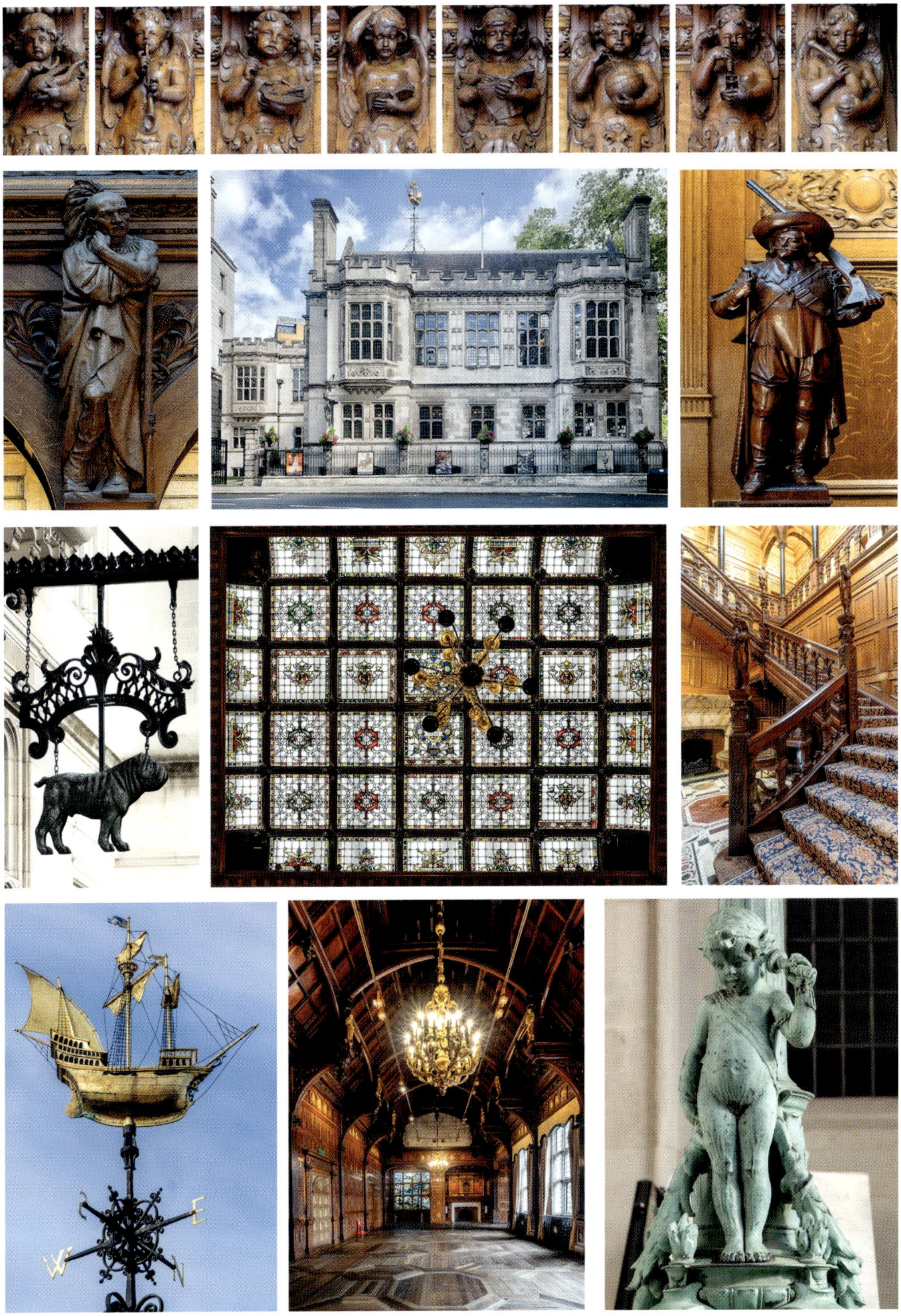

Two Temple Place.

Inside, no expense was spared. A magnificent stained-glass ceiling looks down on ten ebony pillars adorning the entrance hall with a geometric floor of marble, porphyry and onyx. The oak staircase pilasters are decorated with characters from *The Three Musketeers*, and the frieze above consists of wooden carvings of Shakespearean characters.

Astor's love of literature, legends and history abounds in the mahogany-lined Great Hall with its wooden hammer-beam ceiling referencing the Middle Temple nearby (see Box). The hall is lined with a frieze and statues of over fifty literary and historical characters, likely Astor's favourites, including Pocahontas, Anne Boleyn and Bismarck.

Stunning stained-glass windows by Clayton & Bell depict scenes of a Swiss summer and Alpine winter, a link to Astor's love of travelling, but are known as Sunrise and Sunset.

After Astor's death the building was sold and used as offices before being acquired in 1999 by banker Richard Hoare for his charitable Bulldog Trust. Later restored, it was opened to the public in 2011, with free access and regular temporary exhibitions.

What of those external embellishments? The bulldog showcases The Bulldog Trust; the weathervane portrays the *Santa Maria*, Christopher Columbus' ship to the New World, the place of Astor's birth; and the cherubs depict Astor's interest in science and technology, with Two Temple Place one of the first residences to install a telephone.

Address: Two Temple Place, WC2R 3BD
Built: 1895
Listed Status: Grade II*
Public Access: Yes
Tube: Temple
Website: twotempleplace.org

30. HQS *Wellington*

Permanently moored on the Thames below the Temple since 1948, HQS *Wellington* is a former Royal Navy sloop. Launched in 1934 at Devonport, it saw Second World War service as an escort on North Atlantic convoys. After the war it transferred to the Honourable Company of Master Mariners, a City livery company (see Box) formed in 1926, which provides apprenticeships and training to the Merchant Navy as well as undertaking charitable activity. Only the Master Mariners and Air Pilots livery companies are designated 'Honourable' rather than 'Worshipful', in recognition by George V of the great losses sustained during the First World War.

Without a permanent hall the Master Mariners were offered the *Wellington* by the Admiralty. It was refitted at Chatham dockyard and renamed HQS (Headquarters Ship) *Wellington*.

In 2005 the ship transferred to a charitable trust, remaining open to the public, and the Master Mariners relocated to Greenwich in 2023 while seeking a second floating livery hall.

Readers interested in photography may recall this ship from regular appearances in the UK magazine *Amateur Photographer*, affectionately known as 'AP'. Until the early 1970s, AP's offices were across the river on Stamford Street and HQS Wellington became its test subject for lens reviews. These images were taken with a zoom lens replicating AP's layout familiar to its readers.

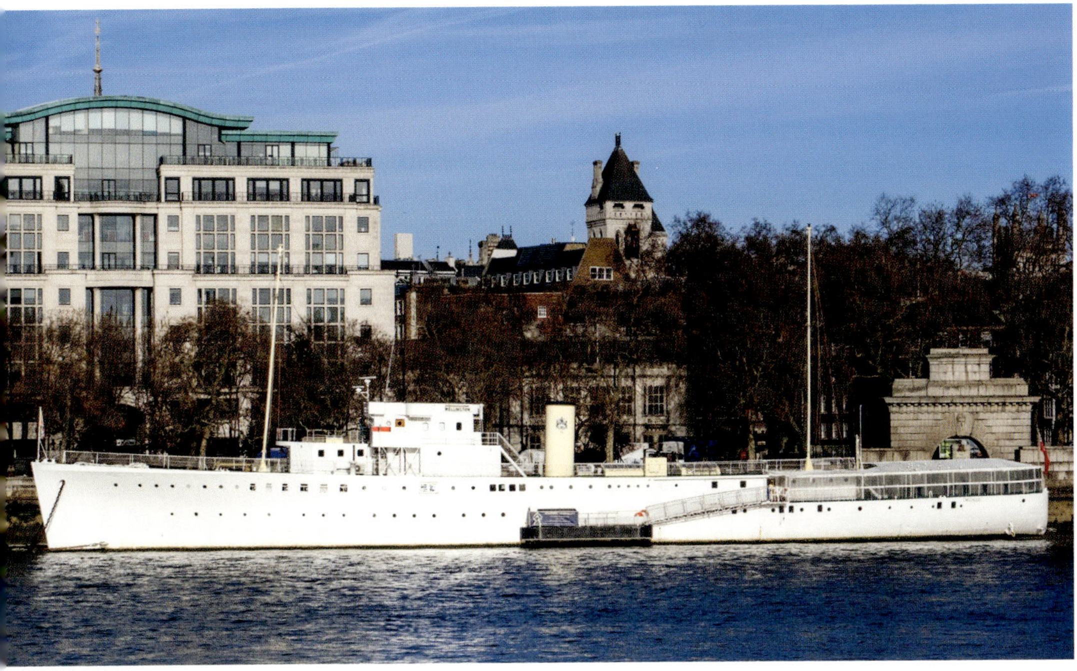

Above, below left and below right: HQS *Wellington*.

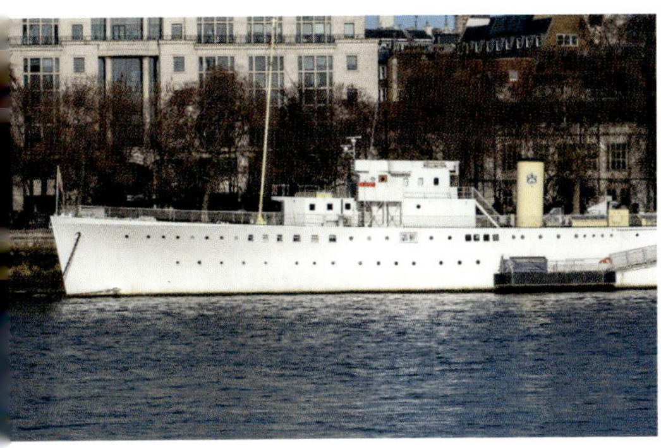

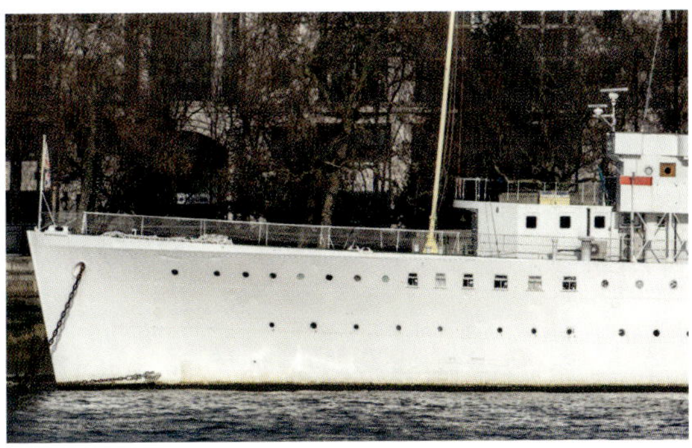

Address: Temple Stairs, Victoria Embankment, WC2R 2PN
Built: 1934
Public Access: Yes
Tube: Temple
Website: thewellingtontrust.org

The Temple

The legal enclave for Middle and Inner Temple, two of four Inns of Court, could easily have its own '50 Buildings' book. Originally owned by the Knights Templar, this site passed to the Knights Hospitallers in 1540 and following dissolution became a centre for the legal profession, perfectly positioned between the business City and the court at Westminster. Emblems abound with lambs and flags indicating the Middle Temple and the winged horse Pegasus signifying the Inner. There is public access to the beautifully maintained gardens, Middle Temple Hall and selected other buildings.

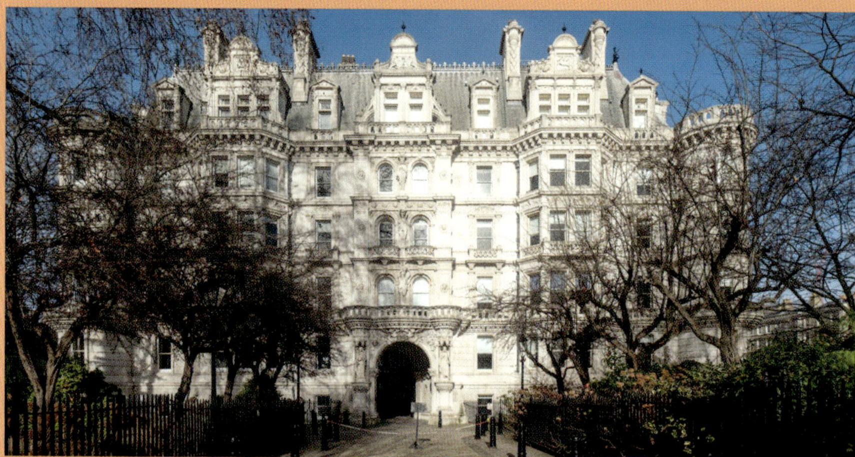

Above: Middle Temple entrance, Victoria Embankment.

Below: Middle Temple Hall.

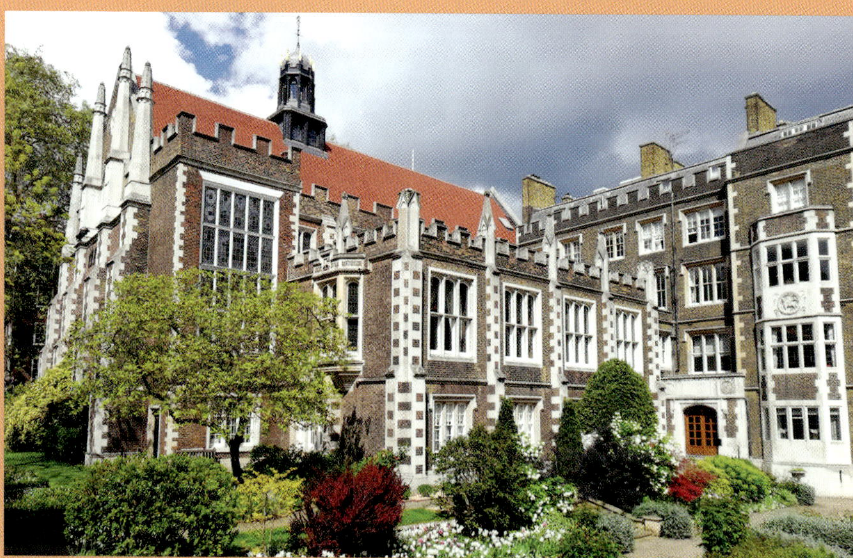

City Dragons

Silver and red dragons flank the City of London coat of arms but also mark various City boundaries. Following the 1963 demolition of the Coal Exchange, two cast-iron dragons were saved and relocated on the Embankment boundary of the cities of London and Westminster. Half-size replicas were subsequently erected as boundary markers at High Holborn, the south side of London Bridge, Aldgate, Barbican, Blackfriars Bridge, Farringdon Street, Moorgate, Norton Folgate and Tower Hill.

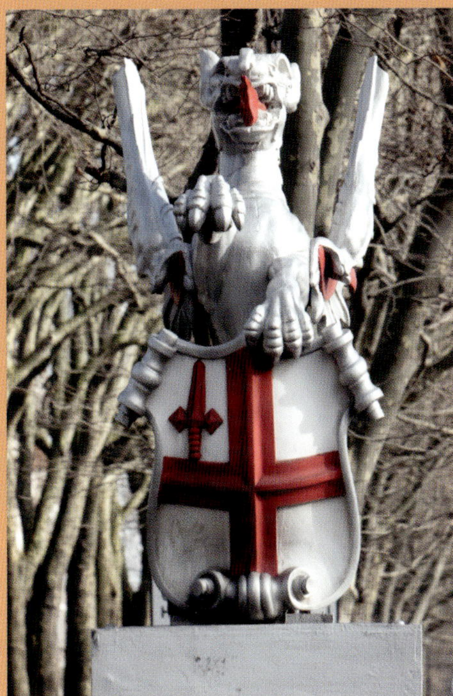

31. Carmelite House

The frontage at No. 50 Victoria Embankment is a contemporary 1990s addition to the original Carmelite House built in 1898 on Carmelite Street. The two could not be more different. The latter is an ornate red-brick building, taking its name from the site of the Carmelite Priory where monks in their white robes were known as Whitefriars. Lord Northcliffe's Associated Newspapers, publisher of the *Daily Mail* and now defunct *Evening News*, occupied the building from 1902, remaining for over 100 years, and the newspapers' intertwined initials can be seen at the corner entrance with Tallis Street. Through the window is glimpsed the recently restored Otis lift and decorative wall paintings. A tall entrance provided access for rolls of newsprint with winches at upper levels reminders of the heavy bundles of newspapers handled daily.

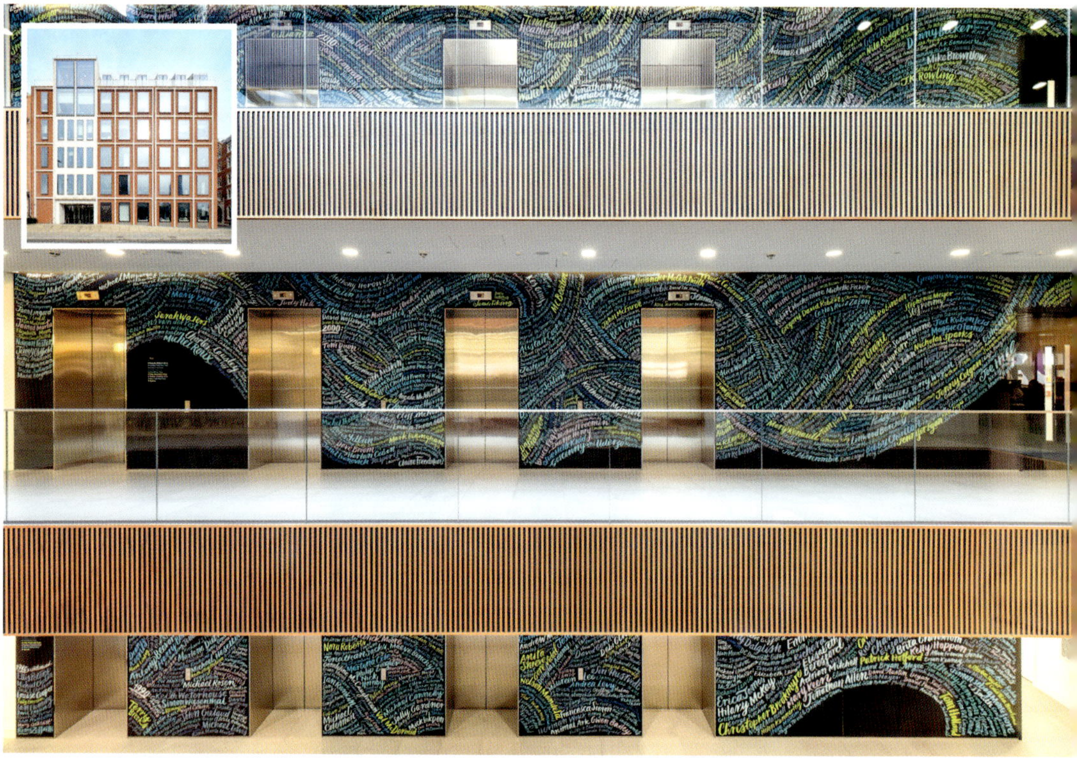

Above: *The River of Authors*, Carmelite House.

Below left: Original entrance on Tallis Street.

Below right: Otis lift.

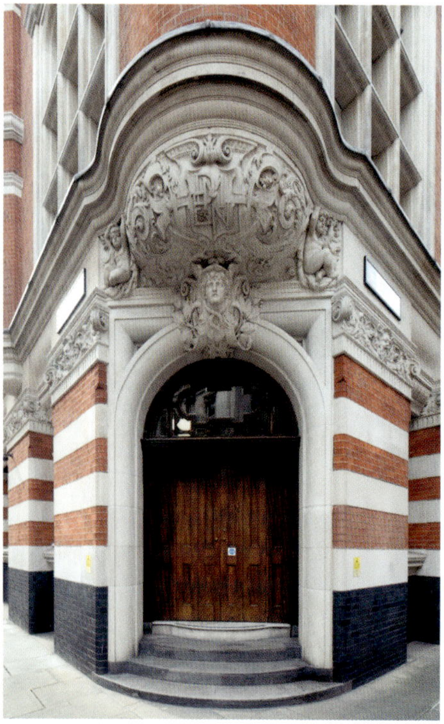

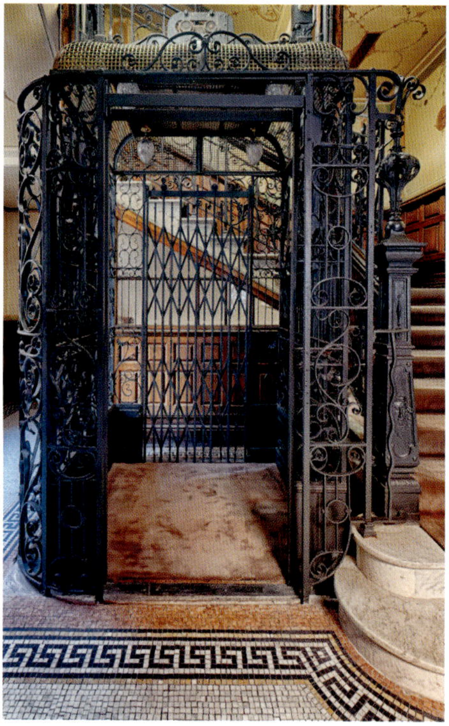

A 1930s extension was replaced between 1989 and 1993, with the riverside and east elevations since remodelled by Fletcher Priest in 2014 retaining the internal structure. The new geometric frontage includes brickwork resembling waves of the Thames. Large rectangular windows and a tall white stone section inserted above the entrance break up the bulky appearance.

A roof terrace with a quarter-acre garden and stunning views across the Thames was added by Fletcher Priest and the opportunity taken to restore the nineteenth-century façade, whose architecture was referenced on the new building with 70,000 long and mostly thin red bricks commissioned from a specialised handmade brick company in York.

Hachette UK arrived during 2015, with all seven of its publishing arms at one location and a company history timeline is displayed along internal corridors. A year later it unveiled a mural celebrating 3,500 of its 55,000 authors through the centuries of the different publishing houses, the earliest being John Murray founded in 1768. Linking to the riverside location the names are presented as gentle waves with this 'river of authors' flowing chronologically throughout the building.

Address: No. 50 Victoria Embankment, EC4Y 0DZ
Built: 1898; additions 1930s; remodelled 1989–93; 2014
Listed Status: Grade II (1898 building)
Public Access: No
Tube/Train: Blackfriars
Website: hachette.co.uk

32. Sion Hall

Originally Sion College, this striking red-brick building in perpendicular Gothic style is surprisingly unknown.

Immediately evident is the asymmetrical design of brick and stone facings framing decorative stained-glass windows with an eclectic assortment of towers, an octagonal stair tower, pediments and chimney pots. The brick frontage of the 1960s ground-floor extension, while lacking an entrance, is punctuated by a series of narrow windows. Three stone coats of arms decorate the John Carpenter Street doorway.

On Carmelite Street, another entrance is surrounded by carved stone masonry including a selection of grotesque heads picking at their teeth and sticking out their tongues.

The building was designed by Sir Arthur Blomfield for Sion College, a bequest by St Dunstan-in-the-West's Revd Thomas White funding lodgings, a hall for socialising and almshouses for City rectors, vicars and curates. Previously located at Aldermanbury and granted a royal charter by Charles I in 1630, it expanded to include an extensive library. but was later rebuilt following damage during the 1666 Great Fire. Centuries later, a more peaceful location was sought and in 1884 the City provided this site with the new building completed in 1886.

By the late 1900s, survival proved a challenge and Sion became a virtual college. The building was sold in 1994 becoming offices and renamed Sion Hall and the valuable

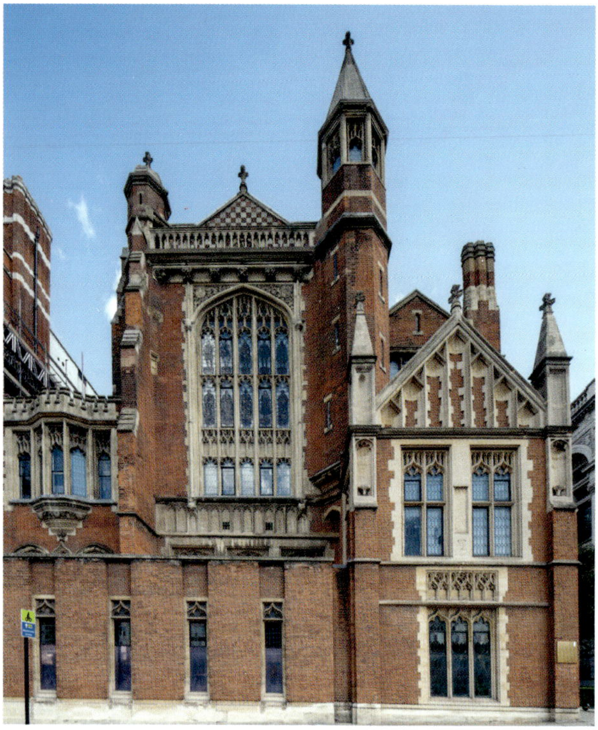

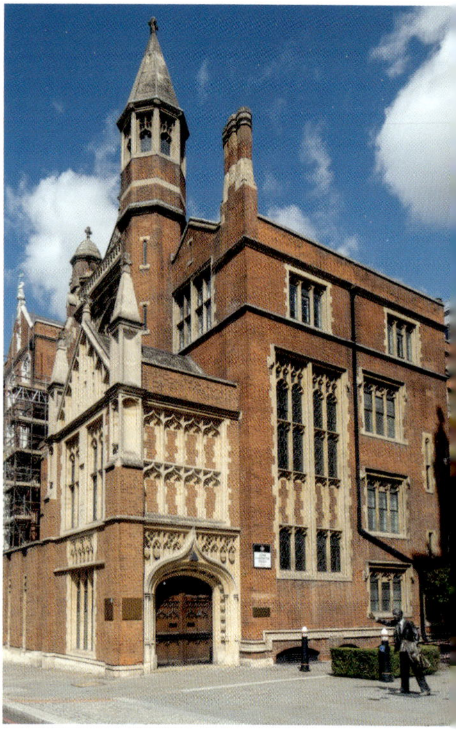

Above left and above right: Sion Hall.

Below left: Front door.

Below right: *Taxi* by John Seward Johnson II.

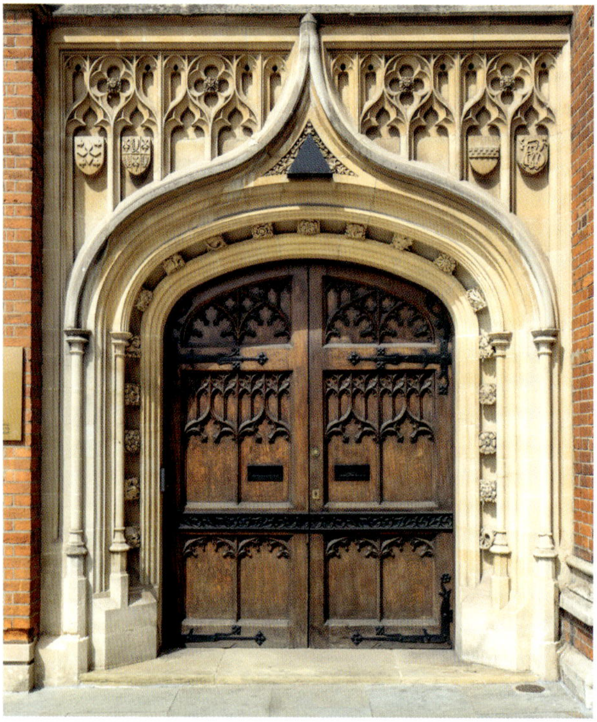

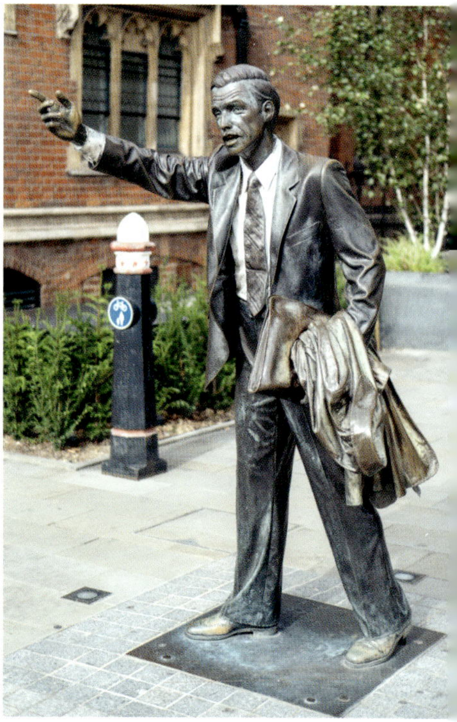

library was donated to Lambeth Palace and King's College London (see Entry 27). Sion's administrative office established at Faith House in Westminster now arranges an events programme for college members thus continuing the founder's original mission.

Address: No. 56 Victoria Embankment, EC4Y 0DZ
Built: 1886
Listed Status: Grade II
Public Access: No
Tube/Train: Blackfriars

33. John Carpenter House

A foundation stone describes how John Carpenter left money in 1442 to fund a school for poor local children, with the first purpose-built school opening on Milk Street in 1837.

Named City of London School and open to all religions, it included science and commercial classes – unusual for the time. Rapid growth in both size and reputation necessitated both larger accommodation and a playground and the school opened on this site in 1882.

Designed by architects Davis & Emanuel, best known for synagogues and social housing, the building embraces several different styles. More elaborate than London School Board buildings of the same period, the exterior features a steep French-style roof of green slate contrasting with white stone dressings. Turrets adorn the corners, Corinthian columns decorate the walls and balconies embellish the first-floor windows.

Four statues facing the river represent literature and science: Sir Francis Bacon, William Shakespeare, John Milton and Sir Isaac Newton. A fifth statue is of martyr, lawyer and author Sir Thomas More. Small windows are bordered by pairs of allegorical female figures depicting geometry and mathematics, drawing and music and classics and poetry, with similar figures on John Carpenter Street.

In 1986 the school moved further east on the north bank, to a building designed by City of London School alumnus Thomas Meddings. This fee-paying school with a generous bursary scheme maintains consistently high standards being in the top 20 for both the 2023 A Levels and GCSE league tables.

Outside, a gentleman is forever hailing a cab. This lifelike statue, created in 1983 by John Seward Johnson II, was brought over from New York by investment bank JP Morgan in 2014, which relocated its UK office here, building a new office block behind.

Address: No. 60 Victoria Embankment, EC4Y 0JP
Built: 1882
Listed Status: Grade II
Public Access: No
Tube/Train: Blackfriars
Website: jpmorgan.com/GB

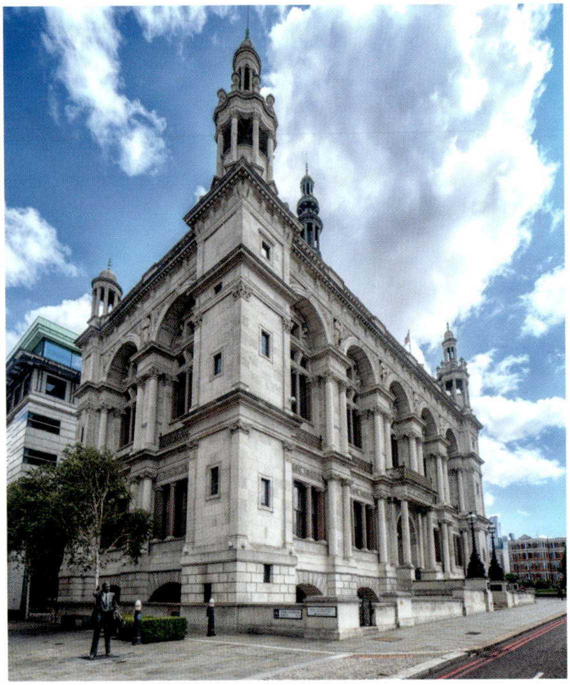 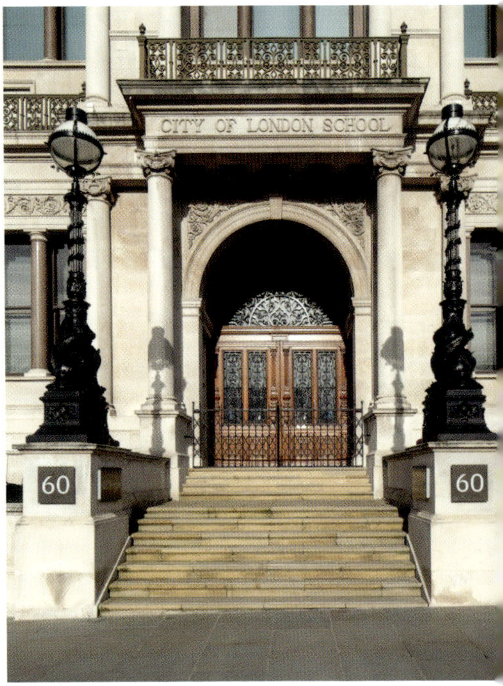

Above left, above right and below: John Carpenter House.

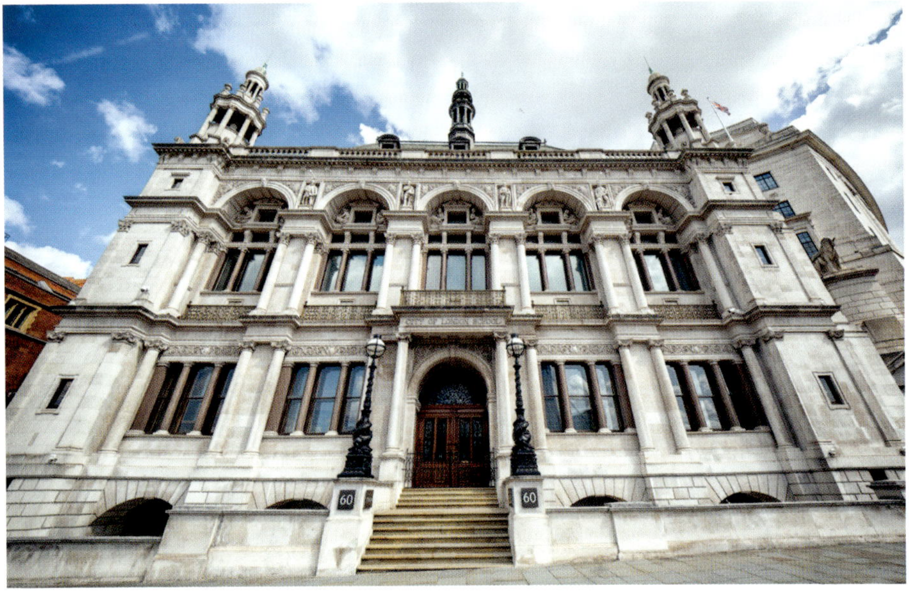

34. Unilever House

Resplendent opposite Blackfriars Bridge, this gently curved Portland stone building in a mixture of neoclassical and art deco styles was built as the London HQ for Anglo-Dutch food processing and detergents company Unilever.

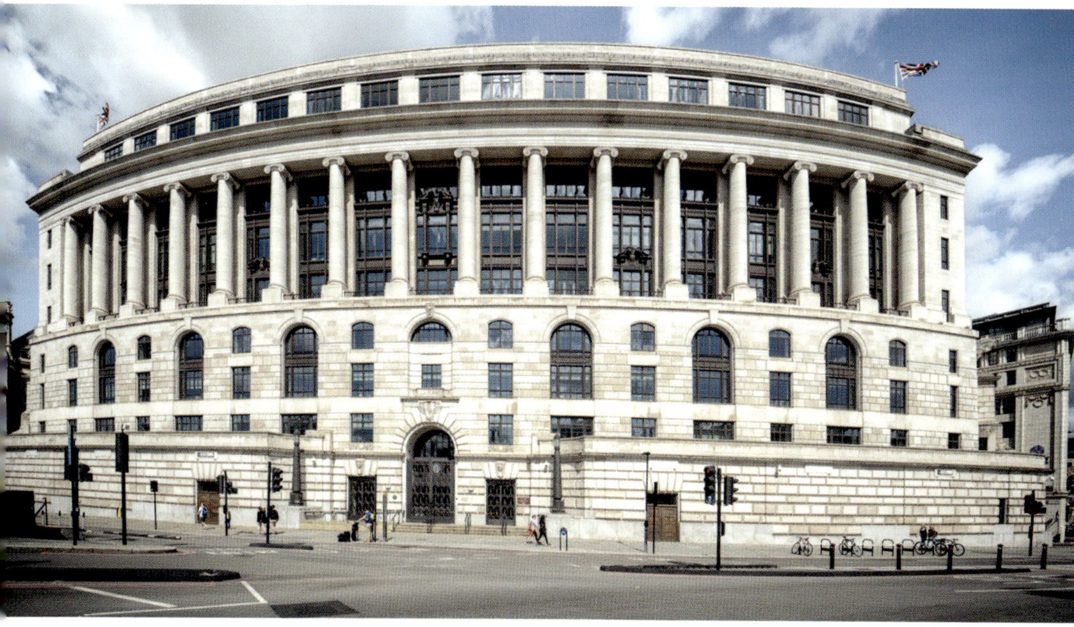

Above, below left and below right: Unilever House.

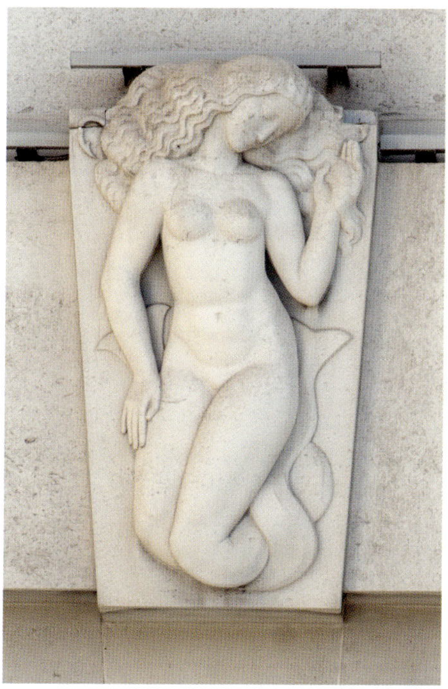

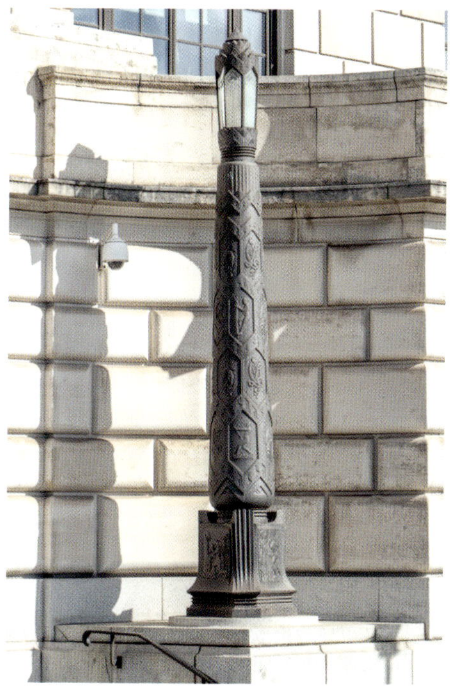

Once the site of sixteenth-century Bridewell Palace, by the 1860s the area was cleared for de Keyser's Royal Hotel, which opened in 1874. Requisitioned during the First World War for the Royal Flying Corps before their move to the Cecil Hotel (see Entry 22), the hotel never reopened. Liverpool soap maker Lever Brothers, founded in 1884, took the lease, merging with Dutch producer Margarine Unie in 1929 to form Unilever.

The grand Unilever House, designed by in-house architect James Lomax-Simpson in collaboration with Burnet Tait & Partners (see Entry 42), reflected the company's size and reputation.

Built between 1929 and 1933, it was constructed around a steel frame with a central arch and two small side doorways. Ground-floor windows were intentionally absent to lessen impact of street noise. Unilever's renowned art collection is only accessible to the public by special arrangement, but the exterior itself resembles a public art gallery. William Reid Dick's two equestrian pieces, *Controlled Energy*, depict a man and woman reining in a shire horse, and keystones by Gilbert Ledward (see Entry 21) above the side doors depict mermaids and mermen. Two bronzed pylons by Walter Gilbert outside the main entrance added in 1932 portray raw materials and plantation workers.

The colonnade along the curved façade comprises sixteen freestanding 10-metre-high Ionic columns linking the fourth and sixth storeys, with urns in cornices above the entrances and stylish art deco lamps providing external lighting. So impressive is the building that *The Times* christened it 'The Monument of Commerce'. Unilever confirmed their corporate identity with 'U' and 'L' initials in stone relief.

Between 1977 and 1983 Unilever House extended into Tudor Street, with pop artist Nicholas Monro creating sculptures of African, Asian and Caucasian females.

Kohn Pederson Fox's 2004–2006 refurbishment retained most of the original exterior but removed Monro's figures. The interior transformation of the interior was far more dramatic, with a new central atrium allowing natural light to flood in.

Unilever remains one of the world's most profitable and best-known consumer goods companies, with 400 brands sold in 190 countries.

Address: No. 100 Victoria Embankment, EC4Y 0DY
Built: 1929–33; 1977–83; 2004
Listed Status: Grade II
Public Access: No
Tube/Train: Blackfriars
Website: unilever.com

35. The Blackfriar Public House

Dwarfed by neighbouring office blocks, the narrow wedge-shaped Blackfriar pub stands defiantly alone. Scheduled for demolition in the 1960s, it was saved by a campaign led by Sir John Betjeman and Lady Dartmouth and is now a rare London survivor of art nouveau pub design.

Dating from 1875 it stands on part of what was the Blackfriars' estate, named for the black capes worn by Dominican monks who settled in Holborn in 1223 but relocated here *c.* 1276. The priory, extending from the Thames to Ludgate Hill, was closed in 1538 by Henry VIII and subsequently used for state occasions, Privy Council meetings and, between 1599 and 1642, two theatres.

The façade decorations and ornate interior were added between 1905 and 1925, while the exterior's corpulent friar on the corner dates from 1983. Colourful mosaics include monks holding flagons of wine with stone reliefs from 1903 and 1906 by Henry Poole

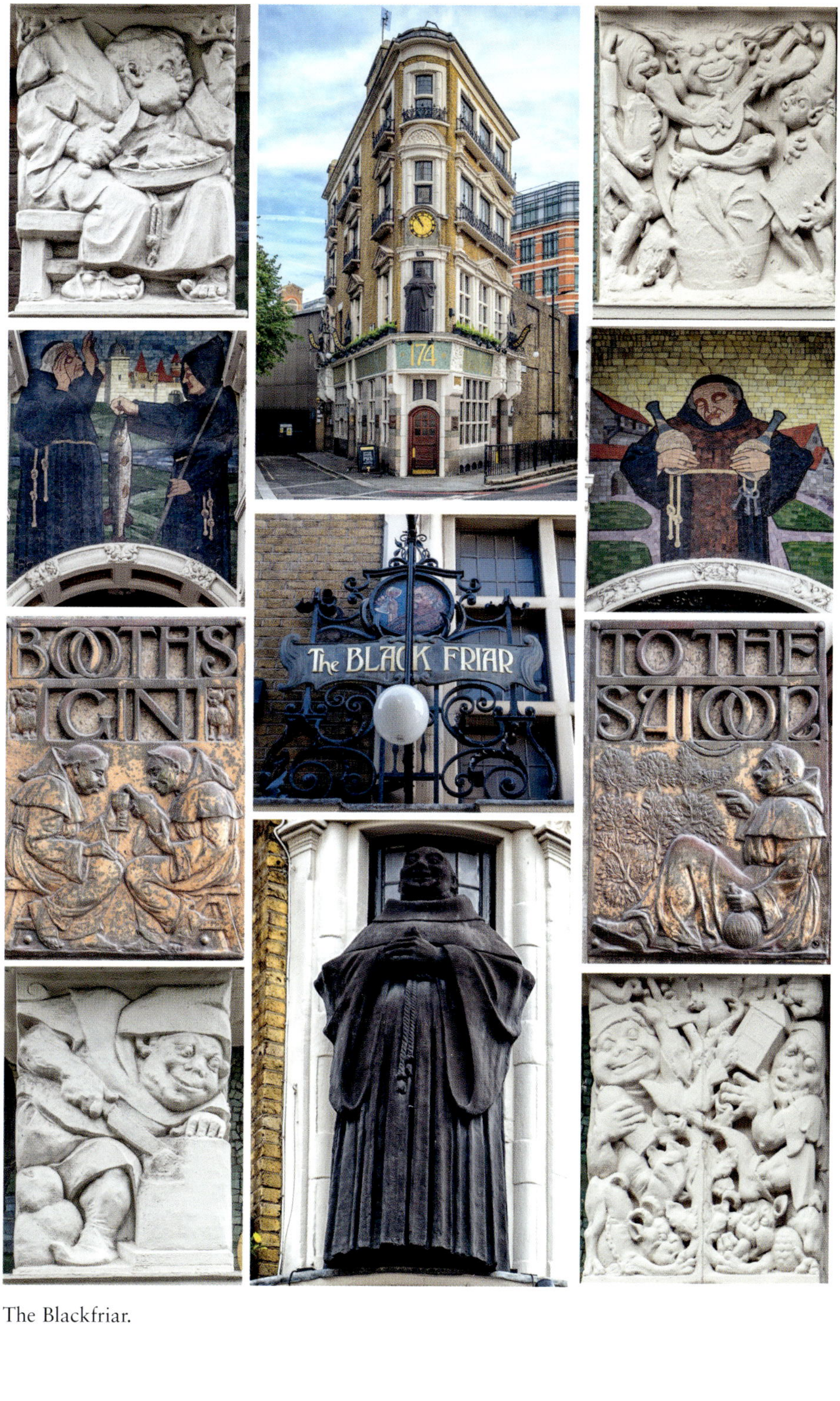

The Blackfriar.

and Nathaniel Hitch, whose work is also found at Two Temple Place (see Entry 29). They depict monks happily eating pies, playing music and slicing a huge wedge of cheese. Bronze signage include yet more cheerful monks pouring ale and opening bottles of wine.

Inside, the saloon and public bars are delineated by the building materials used – marble with bronze and plain wood, respectively. Both showcase H. Fuller Clarke's decorations of copper, brass, mosaics and stained glass, which compete with Italian marble decoration and gold leaf painted ceilings featuring Aesop's Fables and nursery rhymes alongside *bons mots* such as 'Finery is Foolery' and 'Haste is Slow'.

Address: No. 174 Queen Victoria Street, EC4V 4EG
Built: 1875
Listed Status: Grade II
Public Access: Yes
Tube/Train: Blackfriars
Website: nicholsonspubs.co.uk

36. Blackfriars Station

The expansive glass frontage of Blackfriars station at the north corner of the 1869 Blackfriars Bridge mirrors the curve of Unilever House (see Entry 34) opposite. Designed by Jacobs Architects, it was part of the transformation made between 2008 and 2012 incorporating a joint entrance for Tube and overground rail, plus a new ticket hall, escalators and lifts. Elongated platforms traverse the Thames, allowing for 50 per cent longer trains, making Blackfriars London's first station to straddle the river. A new station on the South Bank, the first in over 120 years, created public access to Blackfriars from

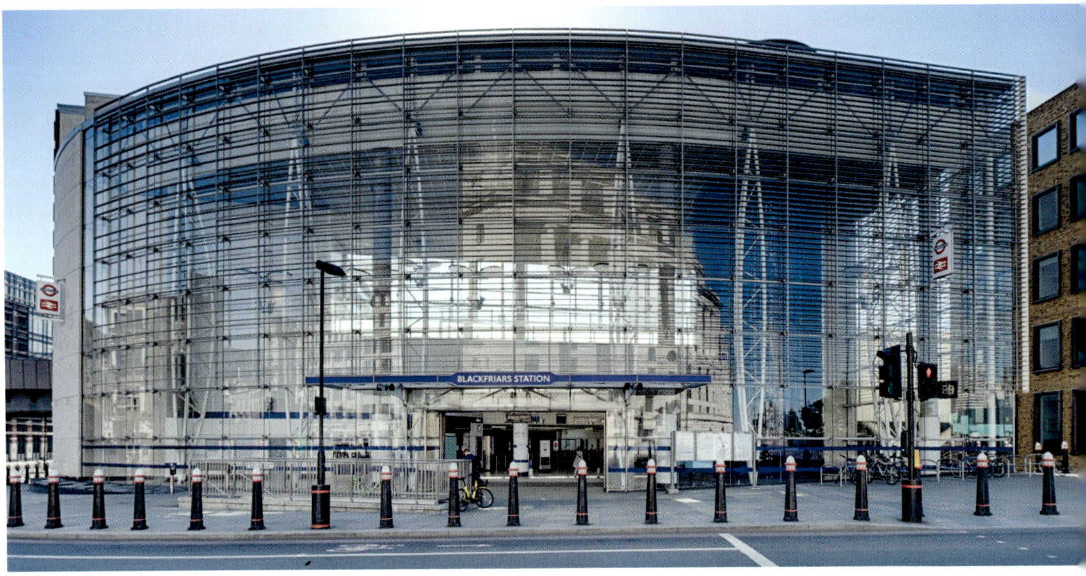

Blackfriars station.

both sides of the Thames. The roof, designed by Tony Gee and Partners and completed in 2014, contains 4,400 solar panels, making the structure the world's largest solar-powered bridge.

The history of the site is complex. The first London, Chatham & Dover Railway (LC&DR) station opened in 1864, designed by Joseph Cubitt. It carried LC&DR trains on its City line from south London.

In 1886 the station reopened as St Paul's, with a bridge by John Wolfe Barry (see Entry 39), the designer of Tower Bridge. In 1937 both the station and bridge were renamed Blackfriars to create a clear distinction from the new St Paul's Underground station.

Both railway bridges stood side by side until 1985 when the first bridge, too weak for modern trains, was dismantled, but the piers and colourful LC&DR crests at the southern end remain. The Barry bridge was key to the 2000s redevelopment of Blackfriars station, which now sits atop it.

Inside the station, a sandstone destination board retained from the building's first incarnation as St Paul's station lists fifty-four towns in south-east England alongside European destinations, tempting passengers from Bromley and Broadstairs to Brindisi and Berlin.

Address: Queen Victoria Street, EC4V 4DY
Built: 1886; rebuilt 2009–12
Public Access: Yes
Tube/Train: Blackfriars
Website: thameslinkrailway.com

37. Baynard House

This brutalist four-storey complex designed by William Holford and built between 1972 and 1979 is often cited as the most ugly and unloved building in the City. Opened in 1979 as a Post Office telephone exchange, it was built on the site of Baynard Castle, one of three London castles constructed by William I – the others being the White Tower (see Entry 50) and Montfichet. It was built in the eleventh century by Ralph Baynard and demolished in 1215, but by 1275 the Blackfriars (see Entry 35) priory was expanding and acquired the site. A second Baynard Castle was built nearby in 1428 but was virtually destroyed during the 1666 Great Fire.

Other buildings followed, and during the construction of Baynard House in the mid-1970s excavations revealed a castle site. Written records confirm several historic moments, including the proclamation of Richard, Duke of Gloucester as Richard III in 1483.

The castle is commemorated by a plaque on Paul's Walk near the Millennium Bridge, and due to the discovered remains Baynard House is designated a scheduled monument.

Situated within the current building's public open space and visible from the street is a totem pole, designed as a memorial to Shakespeare and his theatrical associations with the neighbourhood. Commissioned by the Post Office, designed by eminent letterist and engraver Richard Kindersley and unveiled in 1980, it depicts the Seven Ages of Man from the play *As You Like It*, with heads facing in different directions representing each age and the full text from Act II, Scene VII on the base.

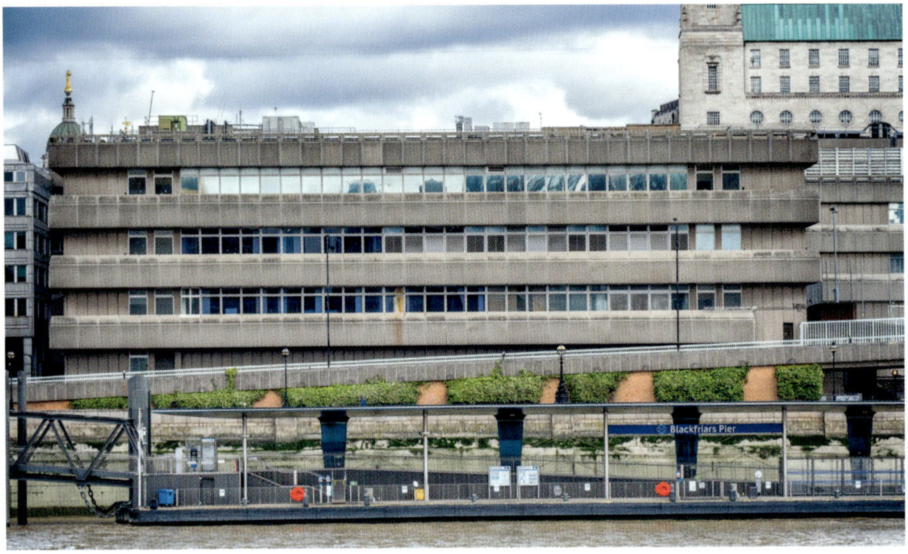

Above and below: Baynard House.

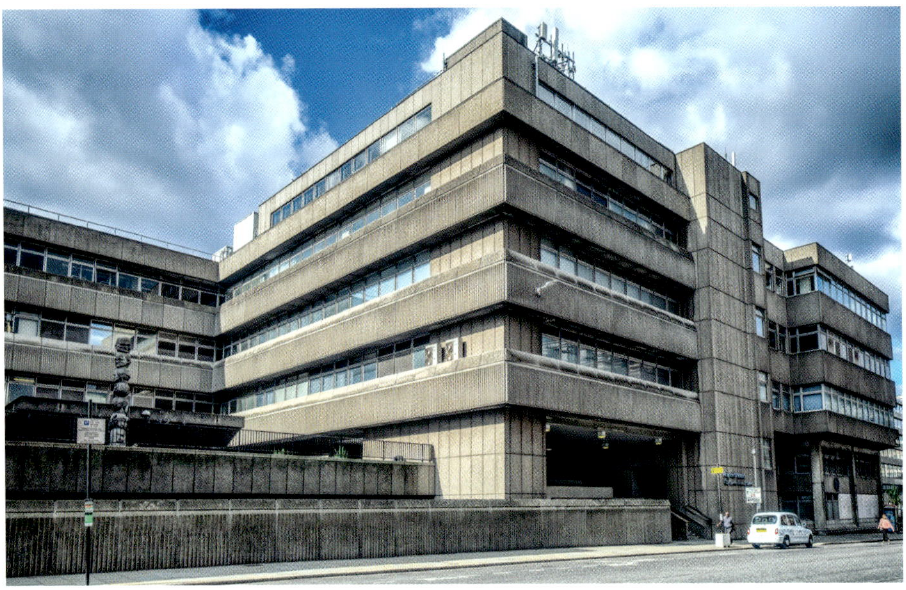

A first-floor walkway, not easily spotted, leads pedestrians at street level via staircases to the external public area for a closer look. The walkway leads to the riverside, rather unexpectedly passing by a football pitch.

Address: Queen Victoria Street, EC4V 4BQ
Built: 1972–79
Public Access: External walkways
Tube/Train: Blackfriars

38. Vintners' Hall

The vast Portland stone building dominating the riverside by Southwark Bridge is Vintners Place (no apostrophe being the contemporary style), a 1990s office and events venue designed in neoclassical style by architects TP Bennett and refurbished in 2017. It fronts the large estate of the Worshipful Company of Vintners, one of the Great Twelve (see Box). On this site since 1357, Vintners – wine merchants – gained their charter in 1363 including a monopoly of the Gascony wine trade. The Livery Hall, entered from Upper Thames Street, has been built and rebuilt over time, the current hall dating from 1820 to 1823 when Southwark Bridge was constructed and the road widened. It was further transformed between 1908 and 1910 by A. H. Kersey, who introduced the north screen wall.

In its current form the hall's roadside elevation consists of two wings separated by a three-columned colonnade. The west side is windowless but decorated with reliefs and mouldings while the east side is ornate with Baroque-style decoration including Ionic columns, scrolls, swags and obelisks.

Inside, a mix of decor from previous halls remains, with the wood-panelled courtroom in continuous use since the 1690s.

The Thames location allowed for easy transportation of wine, which by the fourteenth century accounted for one-third of England's imports. The trade was concentrated in this area, hence the local administrative ward name of Vintry. Coats of arms seen

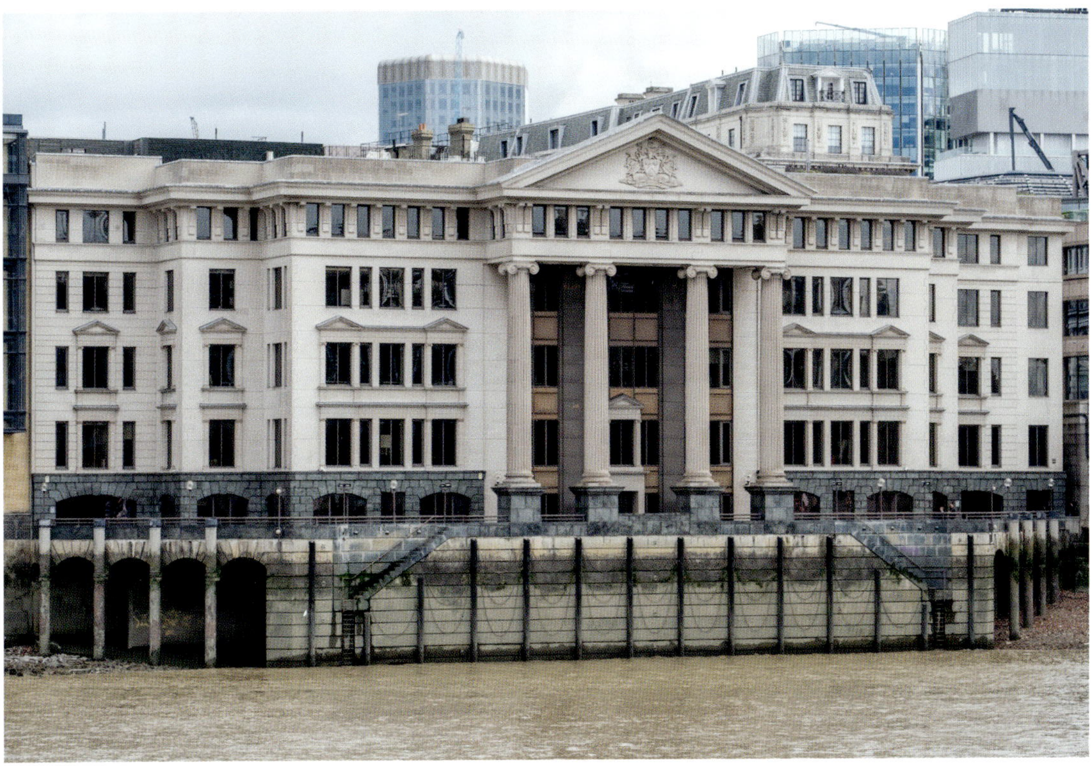

Vintners Place.

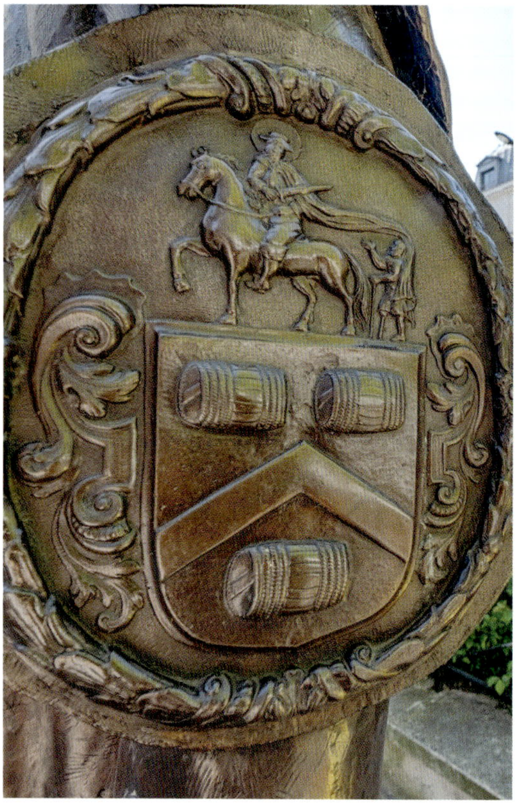

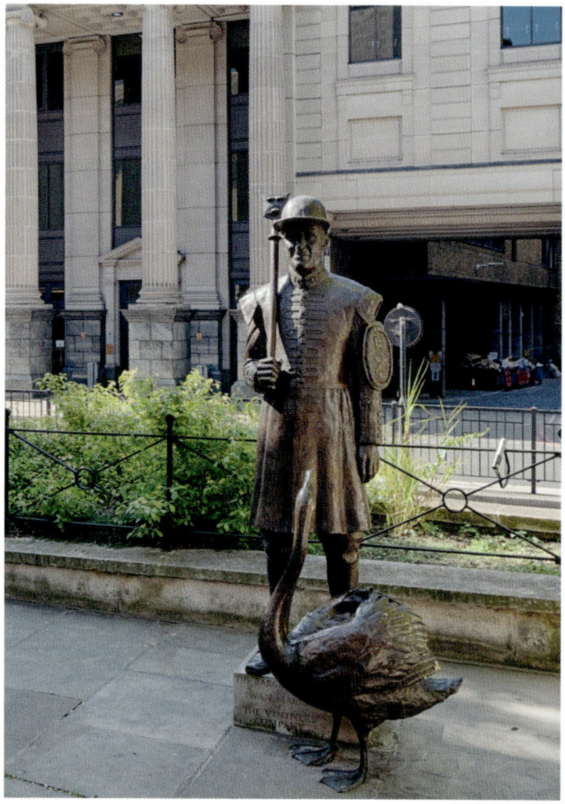

Above left: Worshipful Company of Dyers coat of arms.

Above right: *The Barge Master and Swan Marker* by Vivien Mallock.

above doors and on signage along pedestrianised riverwalks include tuns (barrels), swans adorned with bunches of grapes, and a ship – essential for trade. From the mid-nineteenth century the Vintners' activities became mostly charitable, but renewed interest in wine in the late twentieth century led to the Wine & Spirit Education Trust (WSET) being established in 1969. A new charter was granted in 1973 and two years later they established the Wine Standards Board, subsumed into the Food Standards Agency in 2008.

By St James Garlickhythe Church opposite, a statue of a man with a swan recognises the Vintners' part ownership of Thames swans with the monarch and the Worshipful Company of Dyers. Each July a census, or 'Swan Upping', marks the beaks: one nick for the Dyers, two for the Vintners and no mark for those belonging to the monarch.

Address: No. 68 Upper Thames Street, EC4V 3BG
Built: 1671/75; 1821; 1908–10
Listed Status: Grade I
Public Access: By appointment
Tube/Train: Cannon Street, Mansion House
Website: vintnershall.co.uk

Livery Companies

City of London livery companies are similar to medieval guilds created to support and regulate trades. Activities included apprenticeships, quality control and setting working conditions and wages. Over the years the companies amassed wealth, power and property. Currently numbering 111, most have full livery status, with the latest, the Company of Nurses, admitted in 2023. In 1516 an order of precedence was set for the first forty-eight companies, with the senior companies known as the Great Twelve, headed by the Mercers.

From the early 1700s as the companies' influence declined, assets funded educational establishments, charity endowments and almshouses. Companies have continually adapted to changing times with, for example, Fan Makers and Horners admitting those working in the air-conditioning and plastics industries respectively.

In Dowgate alongside Cannon Street station (see Entry 39) there are three adjacent livery halls, the Dyers, Skinners and Tallow Chandlers.

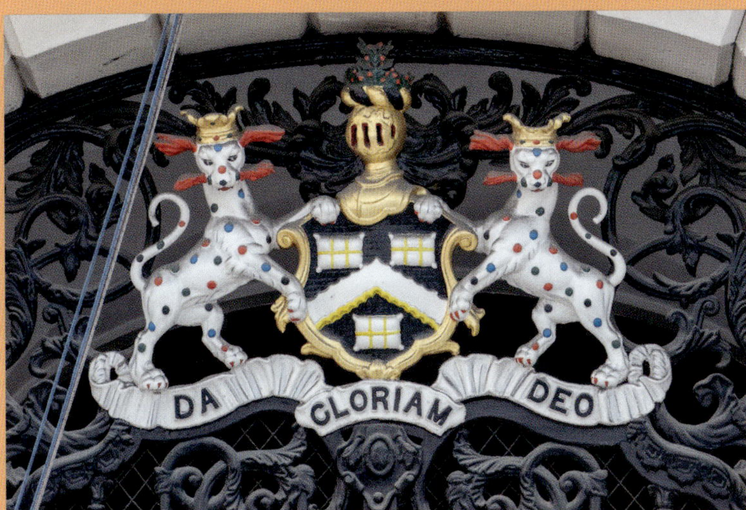

Worshipful Company of Dyers.

39. Cannon Street Station

Opened by the South Eastern Railway (SER) in 1866, the station, designed by Sir John Hawkshaw and John Wolfe Barry (see Entry 36), included two Wren-style towers over 40 metres high. Facing the River Thames and supporting an arched iron and glass train shed over 200 metres long, they survive to this day together with much of the original brick arch viaduct and are now part of the Thames Pathway.

A Cannon Street frontage was added in 1867 with a hotel alongside, both demolished in the late 1950s for an office block above the station. This in turn was replaced in 2011 by the eight-storey Cannon Place, built by Foggo Associates directly above the station concourse. The stunning external frame includes three full-height criss-crossing trusses on the west and east elevations which support cantilevers over 20 metres long.

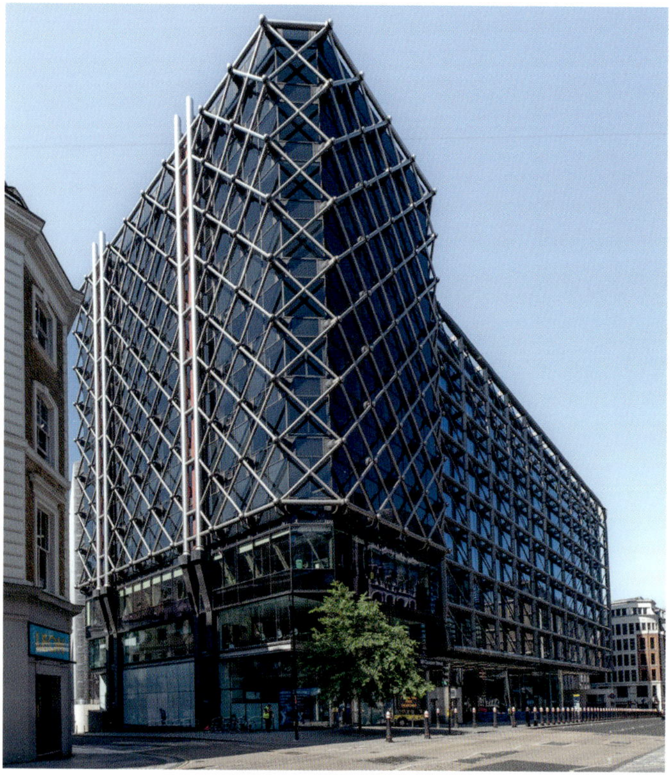

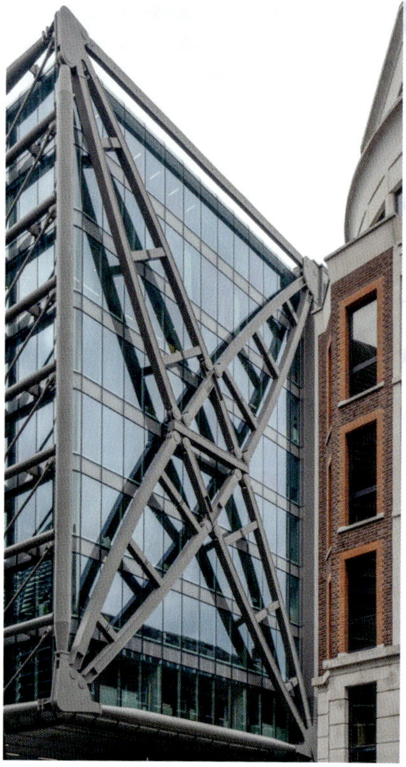

Above left, above right and below: Cannon Street station.

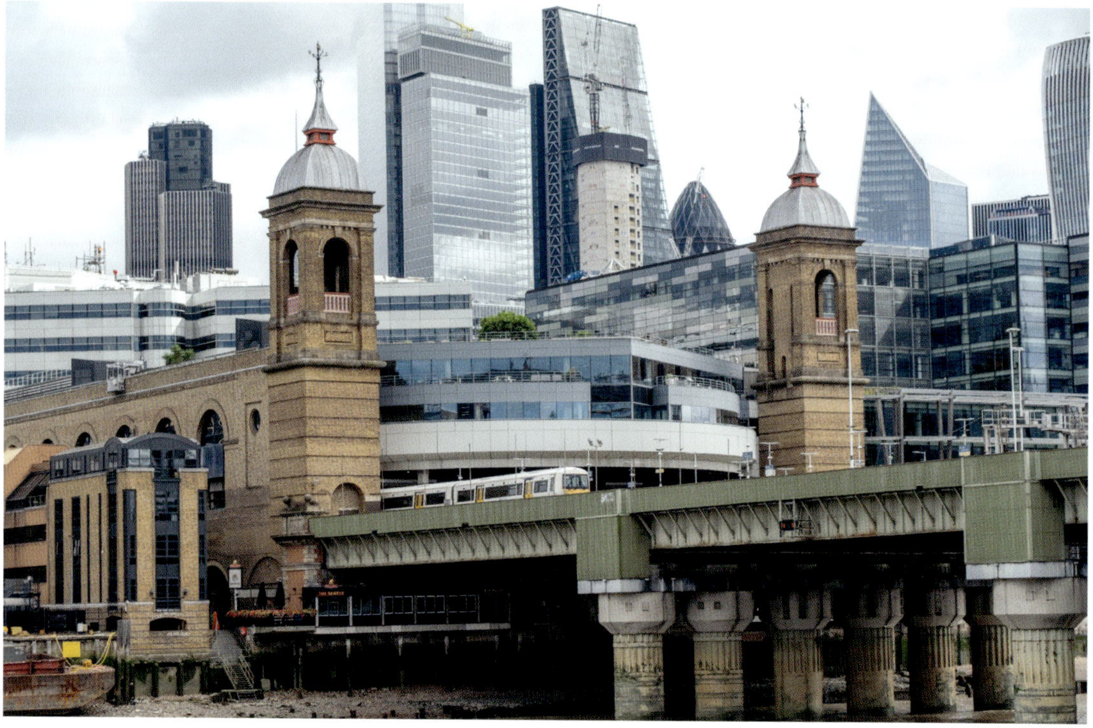

During the redevelopment a Victorian water tank was discovered in the east tower. Both this and the gilded weathervanes have been restored, providing a rejuvenated riverside frontage. Inside, a pub carries Hawkshaw's name and on the concourse stands *The Plumber's Apprentice*, designed by Martin Jennings and unveiled in 2011. The sculpture was commissioned by the Worshipful Company of Plumbers whose livery hall stood on this site until 1863 when the original station was constructed.

The name Cannon Street dates back to candle makers once concentrated in this area. Requested to leave due to the noxious wax smell, their legacy was the road name Candlewick Street, ultimately Cannon Street. The Tallow Chandlers livery hall (see Box) remains nearby.

Address: No. 78 Cannon Street, EC4N 6AP
Built: 1866; 2011
Public Access: Yes
Tube/Train: Cannon Street
Website: networkrail.co.uk

40. Watermark Place

Japanese bank Nomura's London HQ, a vast eleven-storey glazed office block housing 6,000 employees is one of the newer additions to the City's North Bank. Opened in 2011, it lies on the foundations of Mondial House, a demolished 1960s international telephone exchange, with architects Fletcher Priest reusing over 30 per cent of the previous building in their design. The name Watermark Place recalls the medieval waterfront evidenced by an array of artefacts found during a pre-construction archaeological dig.

The architects incorporated more than double the previous public space, with roof terraces and a widened riverside path, Angel Passage, providing access to riverside eateries. This is now the North Bank's largest public space between the Palace of Westminster and the Tower of London. Colourful entrance doors to the offices clearly mark the boundary between public and commercial spaces.

Timber is the dominant construction motif, with huge dual-purpose European oak beams providing both shade and, with ceiling to floor glazing, panoramic views of Bankside.

The greening of the building really sets this block apart from other City offices. Garden terraces designed by Townshend Landscape Architects on the fifth and sixth levels, totalling nearly 2,500 square metres, provide views of St Paul's Cathedral while incorporating secluded seating areas and a cascading water channel. The eleventh-storey green roof hosts beehives where employees learn honey harvesting; nesting boxes, bee hotels and hoverfly breeding ponds were added in 2019. A vegetable patch maintained by volunteer staff produces ingredients used in staff dining rooms. This award-winning rooftop garden, a popular hospitality venue, is the largest of its kind in the City.

Address: No. 1 Angel Lane, EC4R 3AB
Built: 2007–09
Public Access: No; Rooftop garden open during Open Gardens Weekend
Tube/Train: Cannon Street, Monument
Website: nomuraholdings.com

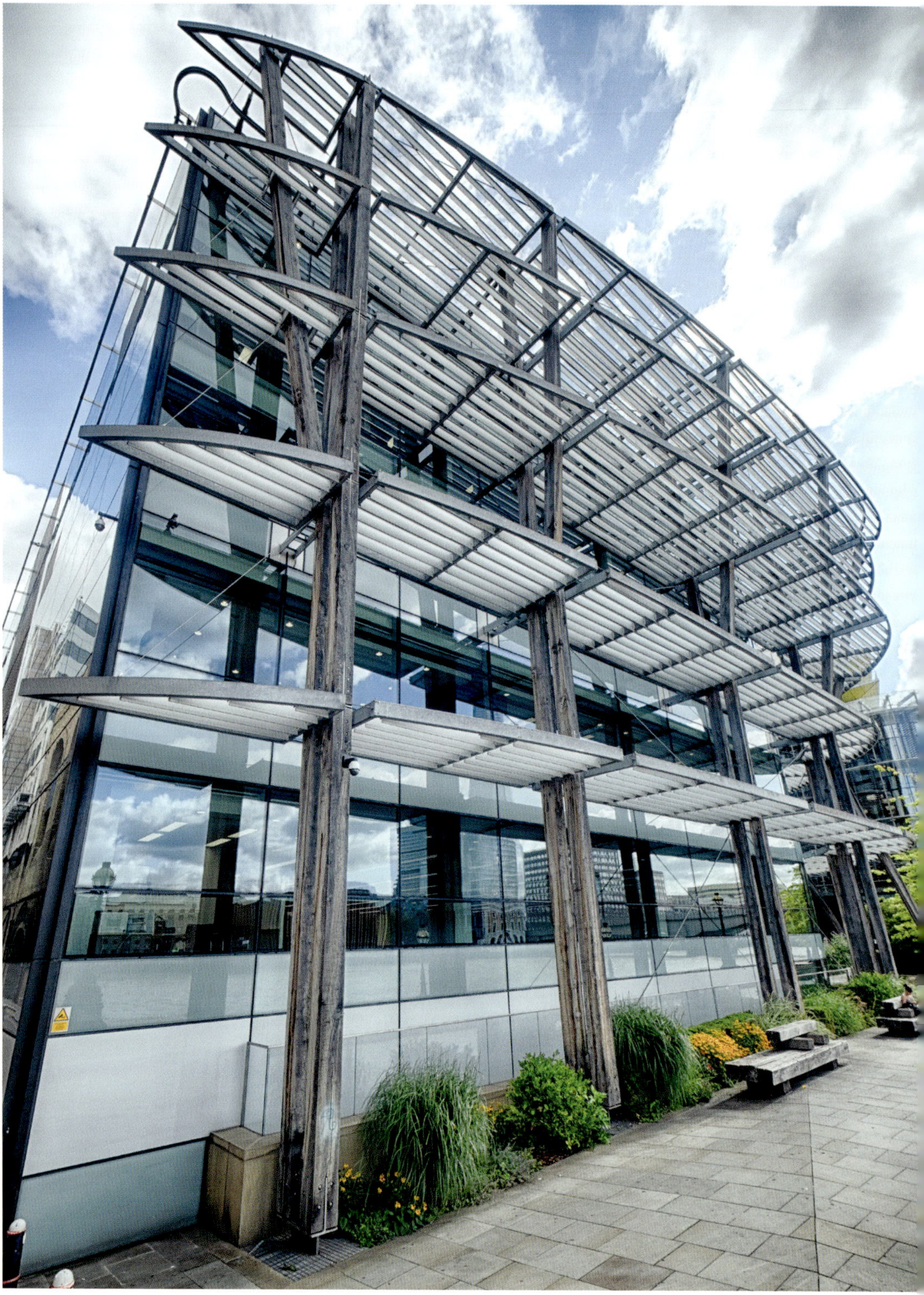

Watermark Place (Nomura).

41. Fishmongers' Hall

Established in 1272, the Worshipful Company of Fishmongers, ranked fourth of the Great Twelve (see Box), has been at this site since 1434.

The hall was built in grand Greek Revival style between 1831 and 1834 by Henry Roberts, a favourite architect of Prince Albert and known for designing artisan dwellings. The river side has a pedimented façade with a terrace and the pedestrianised Thames walkway leads to the lower floors alongside London Bridge.

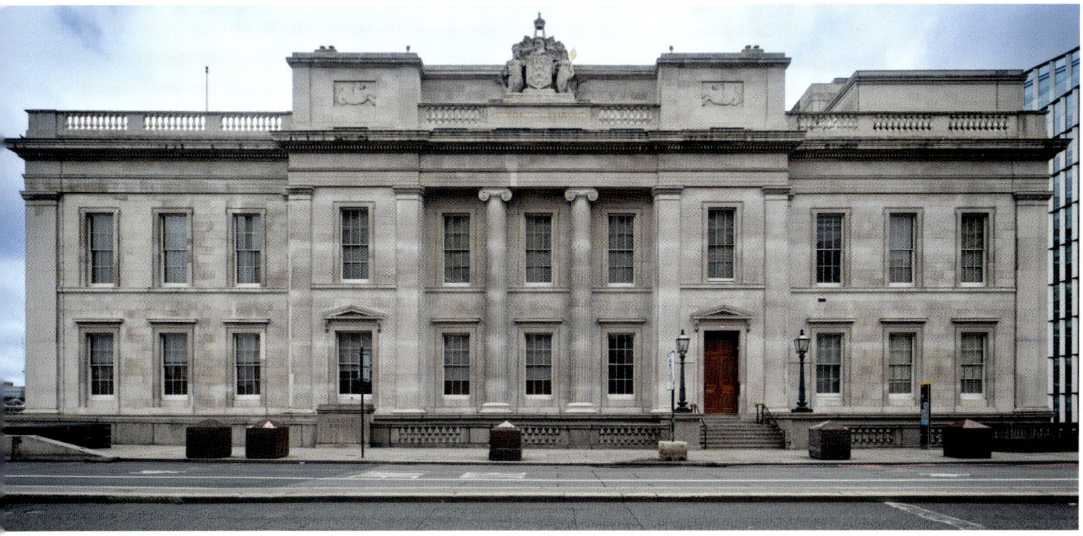

Above and below: Fishmongers' Hall.

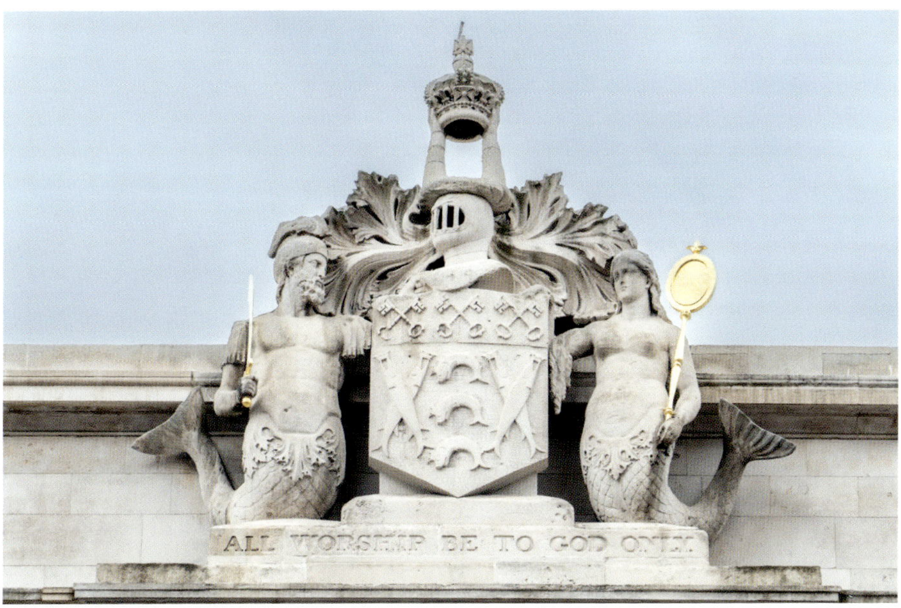

The eastern elevation is decorated with a stone coat of arms with curvy and crossed fish motifs. Flanked by a mermaid and a merman it is topped by outstretched arms holding a crown. Roman numerals represent 1833, with the company motto above.

In 1954, the Fishmongers commissioned a portrait of Queen Elizabeth II by Pietro Annigoni to commemorate her accession. It has since become one of the most iconic images of the late queen and is displayed in the hall lobby.

With Fish Street Hill and the old Billingsgate Fish Market (see Entry 44) close by, the fish industry dominated this neighbourhood. Today the company remains involved with the fishing industry including education, standards and wide-reaching charitable projects that extend beyond the fisheries.

Address: London Bridge, EC4R 9EL
Built: 1831–34; 1951
Listed Status: Grade II*
Public Access: By appointment
Tube: Monument
Website: fishmongers.org.uk

42. Adelaide House

Art deco Adelaide House was named for William IV's wife Adelaide, who opened the new London Bridge in 1831, with King William Street commemorating the king. Built between 1920 and 25 replacing an office block, it was commissioned by Richard Tilden Smith, an Australian who established the National Metal and Chemical Bank for which Adelaide House was to be the HQ.

Inspired by the recent discovery of Tutanhkamun's tomb in 1922, architects Sir John Burnet and Thomas Tait incorporated subtle Egyptian motifs into the Portland stone and granite exterior. Above the entrance's bronzed gates, ornate lamps and burnished pillars stands a sculpture by Sir William Reid Dick of a figure holding an orb decorated with zodiac signs. Below her across the first-floor windows are the seven Australian states' coats of arms. The plain eastern elevation was never intended to be seen, but Blitz damage to the neighbouring site exposed it.

At eleven storeys it was the tallest building on the City riverfront, having utilised a steel frame, the key to rapid growth of skyscrapers in the late 1920s. Interior state-of-the-art facilities included electricity, air conditioning and telephones. Tilden Smith had his own private roof garden complete with beehives, rockery and eighteen-hole miniature putting green, but did not live long to enjoy them, dying suddenly in 1929.

In 1954 the roof garden was replaced by an additional storey, despite criticism for obstructing the view of neighbouring St Magnus the Martyr (see Entry 43). Law firm Berwin Leighton Paisner (previously Berwin Leighton) arrived in 1970, instigating two major refurbishments during the 1980s and mid-2000s.

Address: London Bridge, EC4R 9HN
Built: 1920–25
Listed Status: Grade II
Public Access: No
Tube: Monument

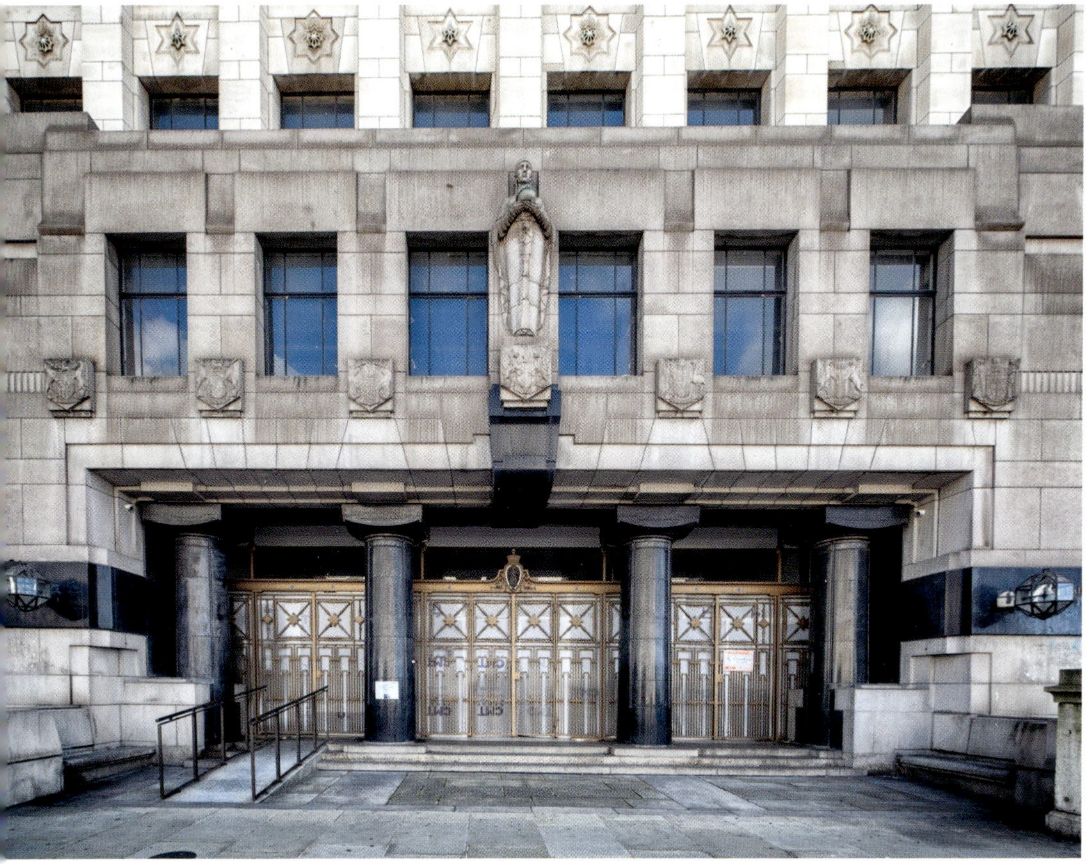

Adelaide House entrance.

43. St Magnus the Martyr

Hemmed in by London Bridge and neighbouring Adelaide House (see Entry 42), St Magnus the Martyr is the first Christopher Wren church glimpsed when entering the City over London Bridge from the south. Its proximity to Pudding Lane, the source of the 1666 Great Fire, led to it being the first rebuilt by Wren. Completed in 1684, it included a tower topped by an octagonal lantern with a lead dome and spirelet. During the 1760s, the tower was broken through at ground level for a pedestrian thoroughfare from the previous London Bridge, at that time slightly further east than now, forming a covered portico for the church entrance.

High on the Lower Thames Street wall a row of circular windows, originally rectangular but altered in 1782, reduced the impact on church worship of not only Billingsgate Market's noisy carts and pungent fishy smells but also the colourful language of the market porters. Swags and panels embellish the otherwise plain façade.

The interior is more decorative, with a double gallery of Ionian columns, the original pulpit and flooring, vivid 1920s stained glass that replaced Wren's plain windows, and a model of Old London Bridge as it would have looked with the bustle of wagons and crowds *c.* 1440.

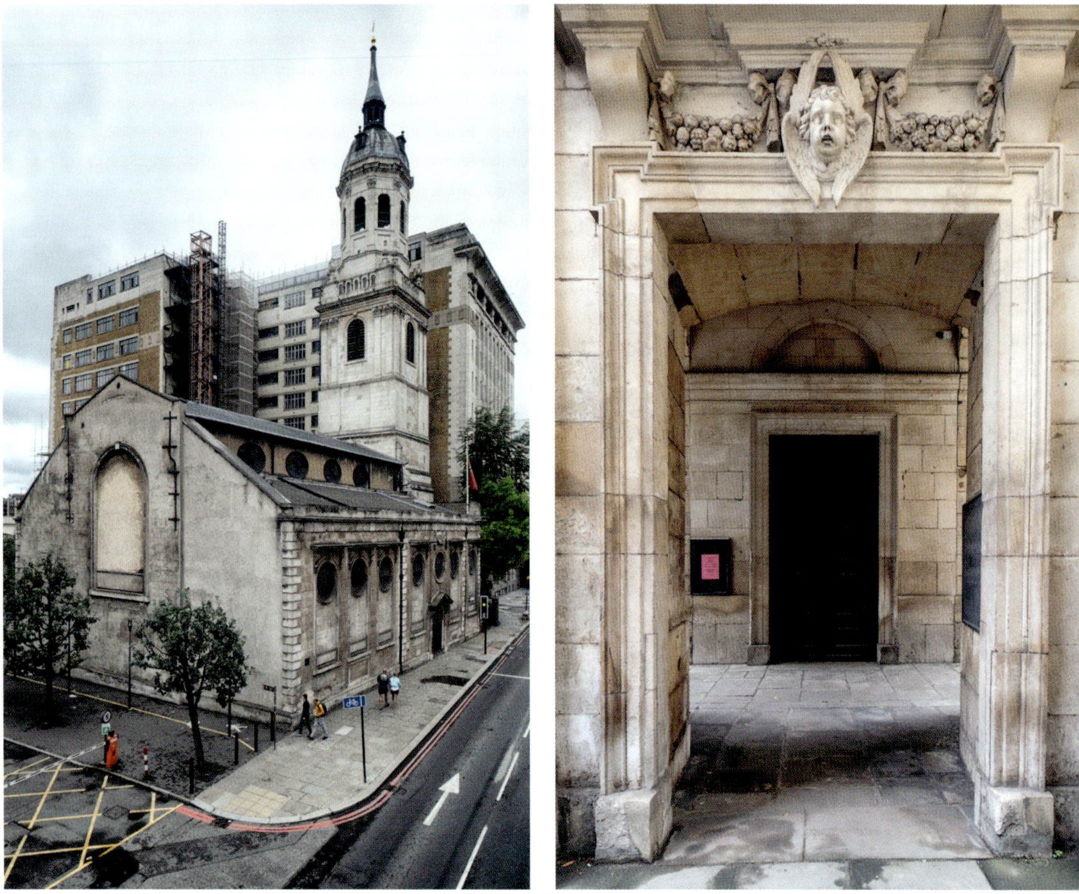

Above left and above right: St Magnus the Martyr.

The splendid projecting black clock with gilt decoration, dated 1709, is known as the Apprentice's Clock, funded by banker Sir Charles Duncombe following his election as Lord Mayor. It is said he was sacked from his apprenticeship for being late so vowed to make a clock ensuring future apprentices would never suffer the same indignity.

Little is known about St Magnus himself, with records variously stating his birthplace as Caesaria, Israel and Orkney, Scotland. He was canonised in 1135, though not as a martyr.

Public access is on a rota staffed by Friends' Watchers, london-city-churches.org.uk

Address: Lower Thames Street, EC3R 6DN
Built: 1684
Listed Status: Grade I
Public Access: Yes
Tube: Monument
Website: stmagnusmartyr.org.uk

44. Billingsgate Market

The fishy decorations on this classical building symbolise the trade for which it was built, Billingsgate Fish Market, an official market from 1699. Despite the name there was no Billingsgate in the Roman wall.

This first purpose-built structure was erected between 1799 and 1800 and designed by George Dance Jr, a prolific architect who built or remodelled numerous City landmarks including Custom House (see Entry 46). Within fifty years a larger market was built by J. B. Bunning, opening in 1853, but increased trade necessitated a rebuild between 1874 and 1877, designed by City of London architect Horace Jones (later Sir), also responsible for London's Smithfield meat and Leadenhall markets.

A wide terrace, once the landing place for fish, faces the Thames, fronting a row of eleven columns with rounded arches within a yellow brick façade. Two towers stand at either end, with giant plump fish decorating the weathervane and a rooftop window. Decorative fish-shaped metalwork within the arches incorporates curvy and crossed fish designs, emulating motifs of the Fishmongers' Company (see Entry 41).

Similar decoration is seen on the roadside elevation, and from her pedestal Britannia would have looked down on the busy, noisy, pungent fishy trade for over a century. Despite considerable growth in local traffic the market remained until 1982 before relocating to Poplar where empty dockyards, pre-dating the Canary Wharf skyscrapers, provided cheap and plentiful space.

Although it is a wholesale market, traders sell directly to the public arriving between 4 and 8 a.m. The current Docklands site is now much needed for housing and commercial development, so Billingsgate is moving further east to Dagenham.

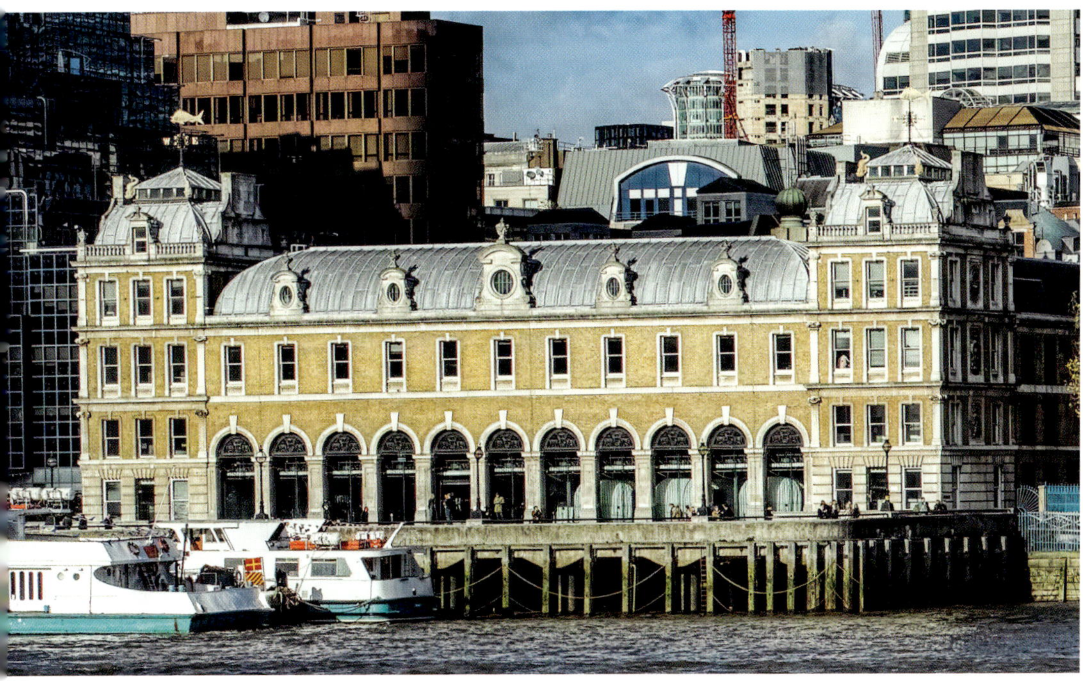

Old Billingsgate Market.

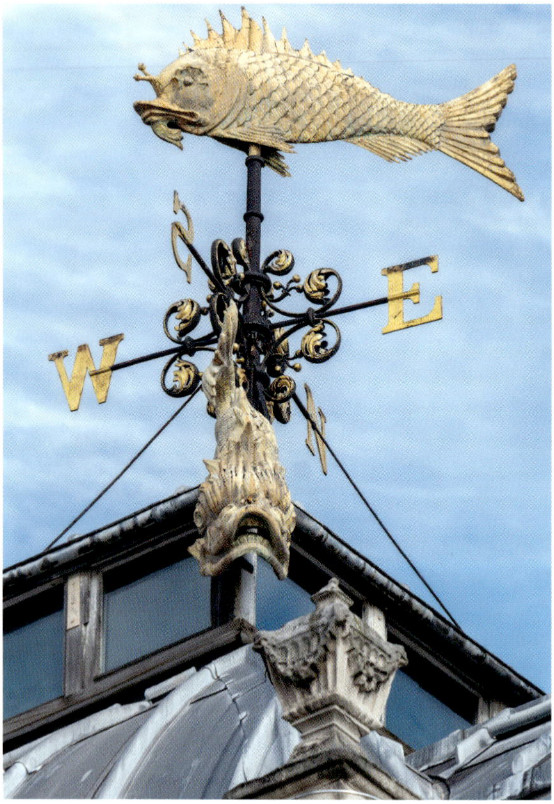

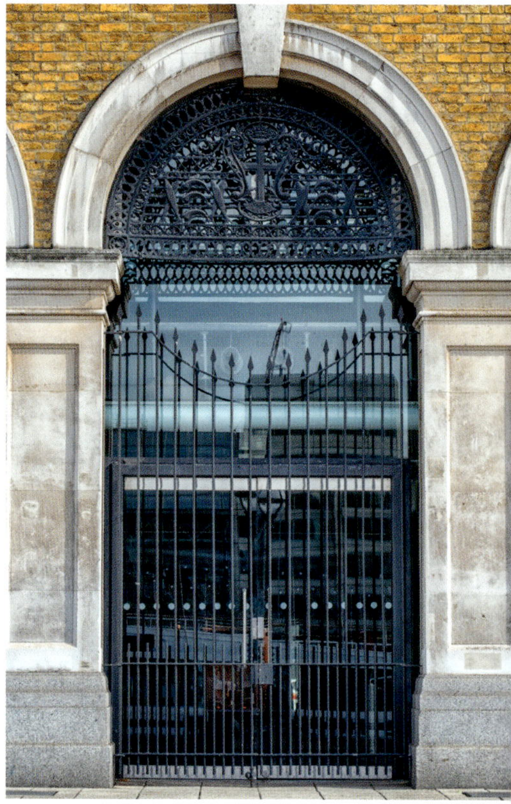

Above left: Gilded fish weathervane.

Above right: Decorated doorway.

Having escaped planned demolition, the City building was remodelled between 1985 and 1988 by Richard Rogers, who repurposed it for corporate hospitality. With a Grand Hall including a new suspended mezzanine floor, atmospheric brick vaults below and a riverside vista, it is a stunning venue.

Address: No. 16 Lower Thames Street, EC3R 6DX
Built: 1874–77; remodelled 1985–88
Listed Status: Grade II
Public Access: No
Tube: Monument
Website: oldbillingsgate.co.uk

45. Billingsgate Christian Mission

Opposite Billingsgate Market (see Entry 44) stands an impressive red-brick building five storeys high with a six-sided turret decorated by four clock faces. Thousands of City

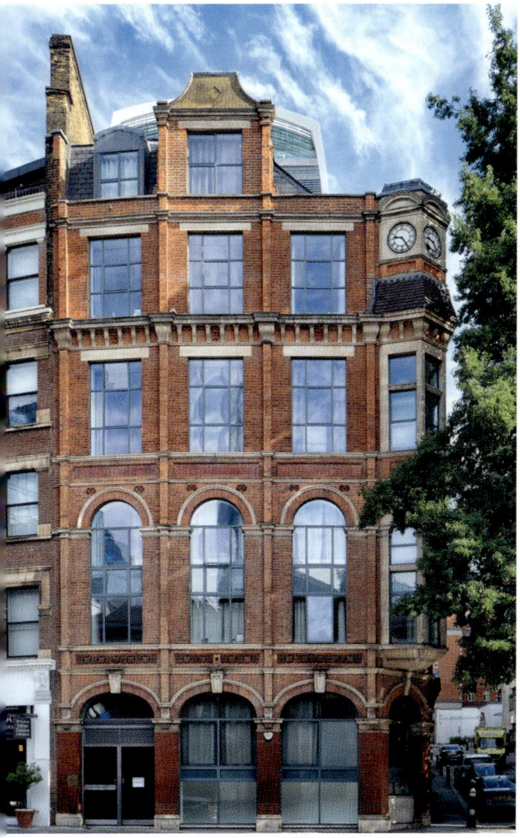

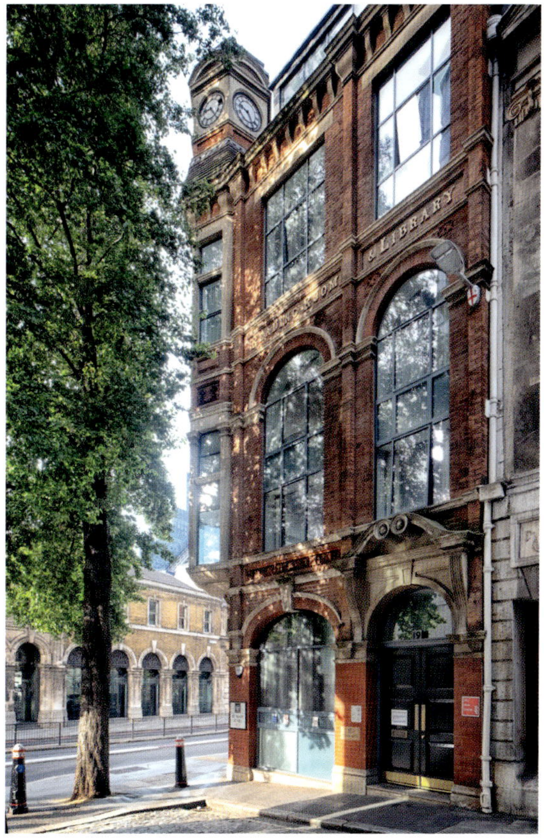

Above left and above right: Billingsgate Christian Mission.

workers pass by every day but never give it a second glance, yet its history is inextricably linked to this site.

The Billingsgate Christian Mission, established in 1878, administered to those working in the fish market. Meeting initially at King Street, as the market developed more workers needed assistance and the charity commissioned George Baines to design a purpose-built premises. Funded by organisations associated with the fish industry and swiftly constructed in 1889, opening in 1890 with a dispensary added in 1897, it provided first-aid treatment to workers, both manual and clerical.

The words 'Reading Room and Library' in large white upper-case lettering on the St Mary-at-Hill elevation above first-floor windows indicate additional facilities, but the lettering 'Billingsgate Christian Mission' seen in archive photographs has long since disappeared. There was also a day refuge, Sunday school, sleeping accommodation, food provision, coffee house and space for gospel and temperance meetings. The ground floor included a post office, with an ophthalmic ward added in 1905. The mission also trained nurses for work abroad.

However, the core function was medical care for local workers, and a 1933 history of the charity estimated that each year *c.* 20,000 people received first-aid treatment.

Despite market trade decreasing from the 1950s, the dispensary continued until 1982, the year after the market relocated to the Docklands. The mission continued until 1990. In 1994 the charitable activities were transferred to the Fishmongers' Company (see Entry 41) and the building was converted into nine upmarket apartments, with commercial premises at ground level.

Address: No. 53 Monument Street, EC3R 8BU
Built: 1889/90
Public Access: No
Tube: Monument

46. Custom House

This 140-metre-long white Portland stone frontage dominating the riverfront is Custom House, currently empty and awaiting approval for redevelopment. However, for centuries this building was a hive of activity, checking cargoes, assessing taxes and duties and registering immigrants and emigrants. With the first recorded tax dated 743, His Majesty's Revenue & Customs (HMRC), is one of the world's oldest tax-collecting agencies, with taxes on wool, hair powder, wallpaper, gloves, vinegar and hats all levied at some point.

Wool Quay, an early collection point, was superseded by an enlarged Custom House in 1559. Destroyed by the 1666 Great Fire, it was rebuilt by Sir Christopher Wren who introduced a Long Room for the desk clerks, an architectural feature included in all subsequent customs houses on this site. Following two further fires, a rebuild by David Laing (see Entry 47) in 1817, and then subsidence, Robert Smirke (see Entry 24) remodelled the building in the late 1820s, with John Rennie constructing Custom House Quay

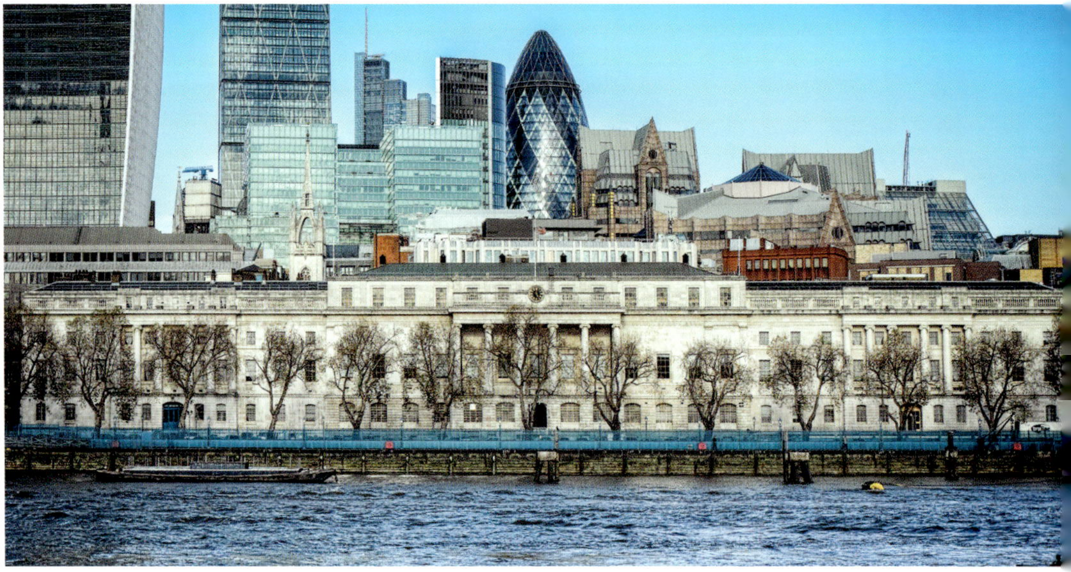

Custom House.

alongside. Smirke's Long Room, 58 metres long, 19 metres wide and over 16 metres high, remains to this day. Inside, surviving features from Laing's rebuild include a weathervane repeater and an expansive robing room.

Administering customs and excise requires attention to detail and employees were both numerate and literate. Several staff went on to become famous authors, including Geoffrey Chaucer, Robbie Burns and William Wordsworth. In the late nineteenth century, customs was one of the first civil service departments to employ women, many as search officers.

Despite facing increasing challenges such as the introduction of VAT in 1973, drug smuggling and trade in ivory and endangered species resulting in a substantial 1992 refurbishment, HMRC vacated the building in 2021.

Custom House is now a work in progress. Recommendations for future use include the Long Room becoming a multi-use space with public access to the riverside terrace via a link from Lower Thames Street through the King's Warehouse, a columned hall built to store confiscated goods.

Address: No. 101 Lower Thames Street, EC3R 6DL
Built: 1814–1817; remodelled 1825–27
Listed Status: Grade I
Public Access: No
Tube: Monument, Tower Hill

47. St Dunstan in the East

Standing within the gardens of St Dunstan in the East, where ivy and creepers climb sinuously through empty stone window tracery, visitors could be forgiven for thinking they had stumbled upon a stage set for an old Gothic ruin. The tower and steeple, however, are reminders of a church built possibly around 950 by St Dunstan, Bishop of London and later Archbishop of Canterbury. Two City churches were named in his honour, differentiated by suffixes East and West, the latter still in use on Fleet Street.

This eastern parish grew rapidly and proximity to Billingsgate Market and Custom House (see Entries 44, 46) brought wealth and prestige, with the minister receiving the second highest stipend in the City after St Magnus the Martyr (see Entry 43).

Extensive repairs in 1633 were followed by severe damage during the 1666 Great Fire. Between 1668 and 1701 the church was rebuilt in a Gothic style by Sir Christopher Wren, with his daughter Jane assisting with the steeple. Despite the apparent fragility and weightlessness of the slender spire, with its pinnacles and flying buttresses, it was built to last and even survived a hurricane in 1703. However, the nave walls were not as strong and the pressure of the roof pushed them outwards, necessitating another rebuild. Between 1817 and 1821 David Laing (see Entry 46) refurbished it in the Gothic Revival style while incorporating Wren's tower and spire, which remain today.

By 1941, with the City population decreasing rapidly, the church became a chapel of ease, providing access to worship for those living in a large parish but far from the main church. Following extensive Blitz damage the same year, it was not rebuilt and the site was transformed in 1967 into this atmospheric public garden, incorporating a fig tree planted in 1937 to commemorate George VI's coronation. Since officially opening in 1971 the

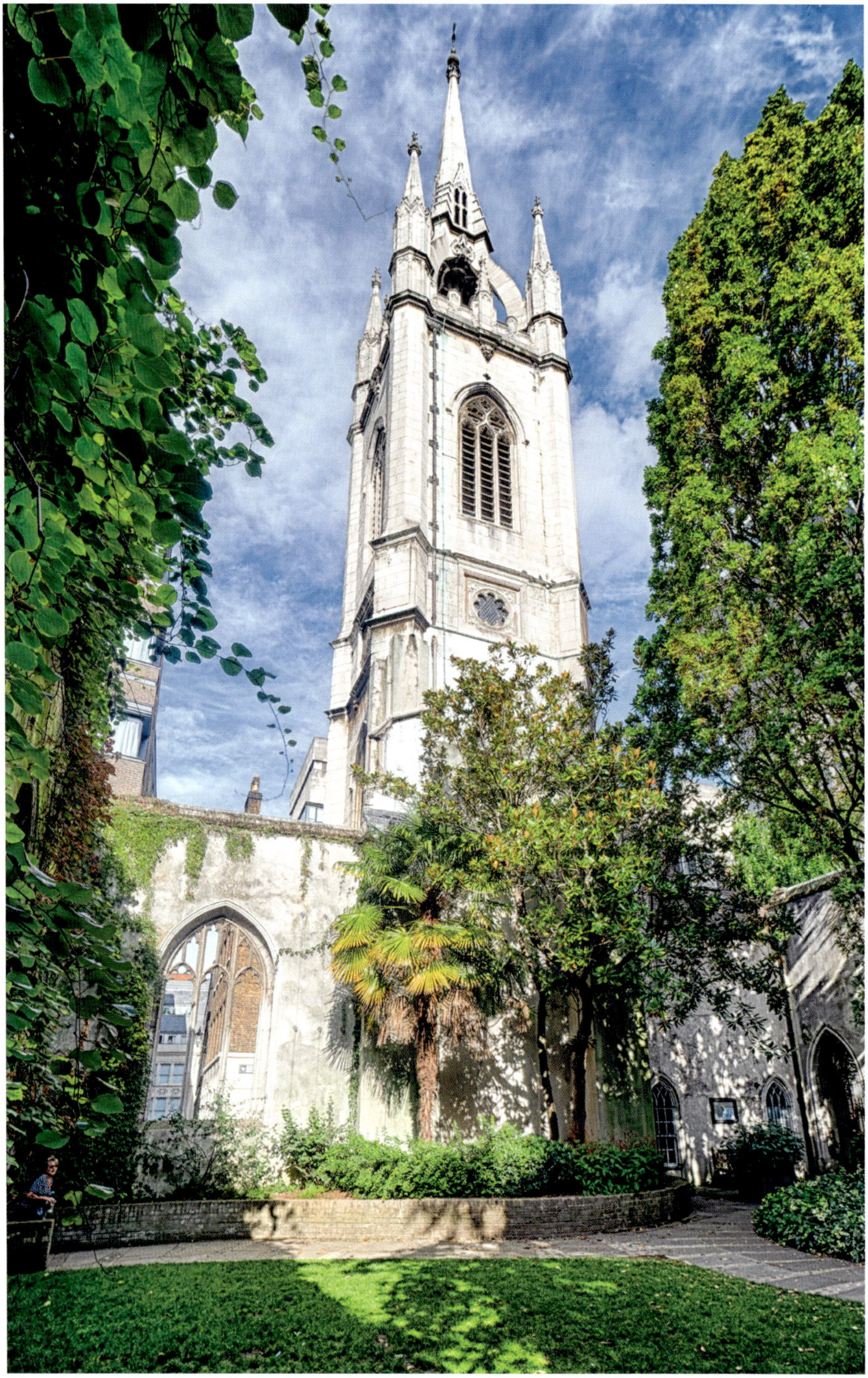

St Dunstan in the East Church Garden.

garden has continued to grow in popularity, becoming one of the most 'Instagrammable' in the City.

Address: St Dunstan's Hill, EC3R 5DD
Built: 1668–1701; 1817–21
Listed Status: Grade I
Public Access: Yes
Tube: Monument, Tower Hill

48. No. 10 Trinity Square

Overlooking Tower Hill, this immense white Portland stone edifice, currently a luxury hotel, was built as the HQ for the Port of London Authority (PLA). Formed in 1909, the PLA amalgamated the several London dock companies into a cohesive and co-ordinated body administering over 150 km of tidal Thames, focusing on river safely and navigation.

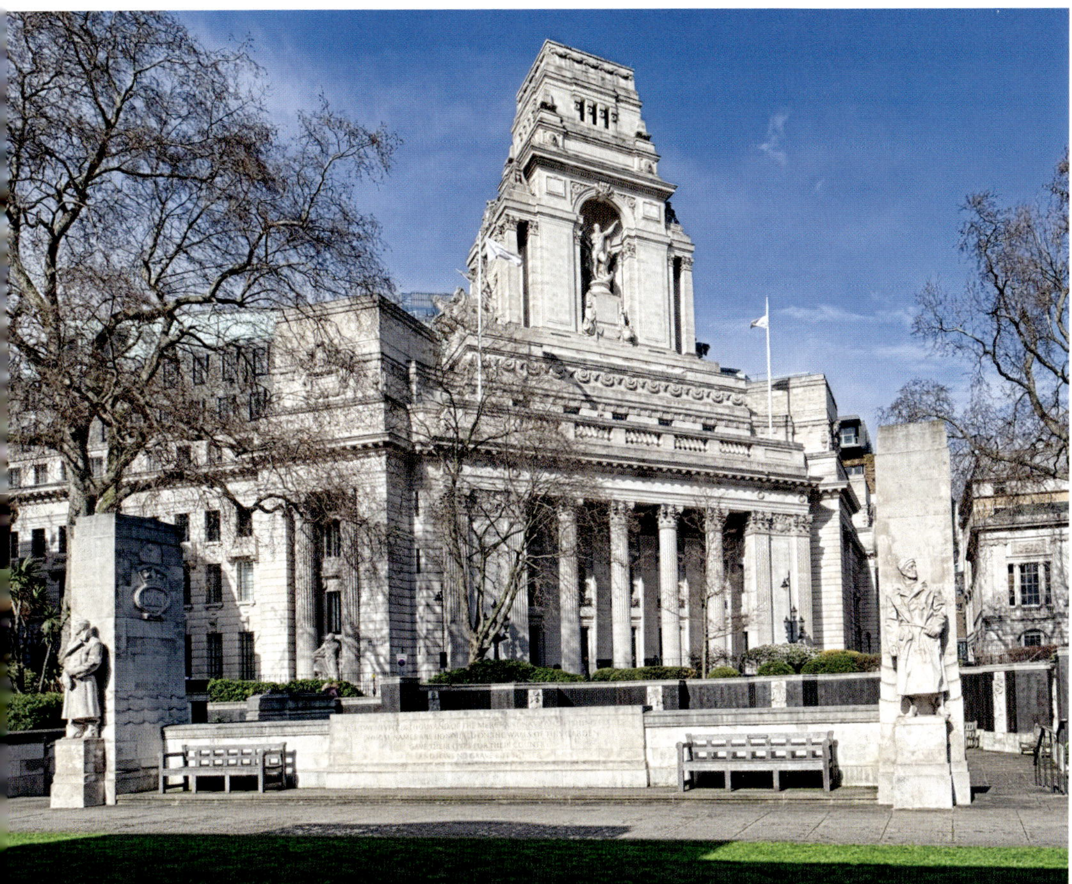

Former Port of London Authority, now No. 10 Trinity Square.

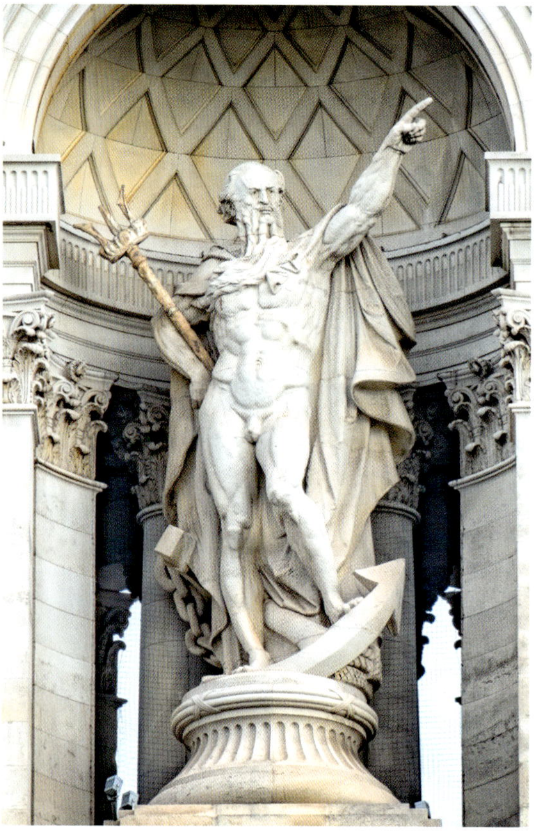

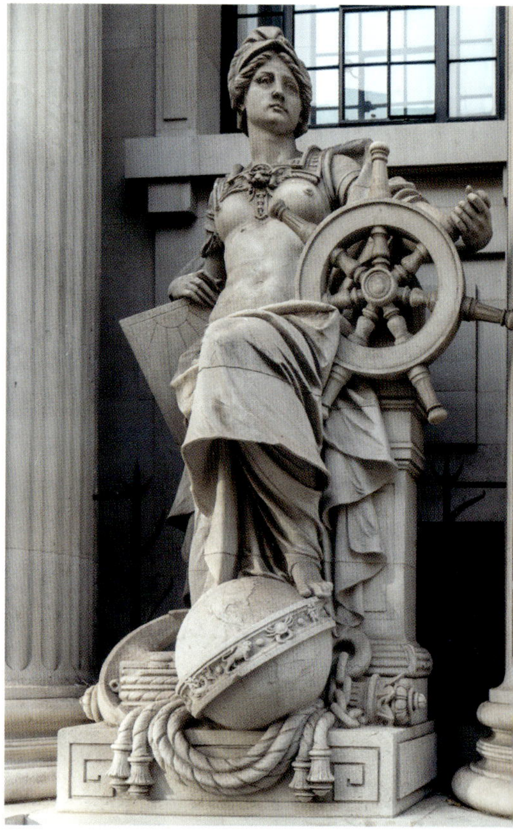

Above left: *Old Father Thames* (based on Neptune).

Above right: *Navigation*.

Sir Edwin Cooper won the commission with an elaborate Beaux-Arts design. It was completed in 1922 and opened by Prime Minister Lloyd George, President of the Board of Trade, when the PLA was established. The prestige of the building was assured when used for the inaugural meeting of the United Nations in 1946.

Nautical associations abound. The sides of the building align to the points of the compass. From the tower a bearded statue of Old Father Thames, complete with trident and anchor, looks towards the river. Within the tower were four rooms, one on top of the other, accessed by an iron spiral staircase. Four statues by Alfred Hodge (see Entry 7) symbolise Produce, Husbandry (represented by oxen led by a chariot) and Exportation, a ship led by sea horses and steered by Prowess. When Hodge died in 1917 his protégée Charles Dolman added figures representing Commerce and Navigation. The maritime associations continue in Trinity Square Gardens, with First and Second World War Merchant Navy memorials.

The 20.5-metre-high rotunda destroyed by the Blitz and replaced by a new wing in the 1970s has been reinstated and is visible from the entrance.

The PLA relocated to Tilbury in 1970, replaced by insurance broker Willis Faber (later Willis Corroon and currently Willis Towers Watson) until they moved three decades later to purpose-built offices opposite Lloyds of London. In 2017 the Four Seasons Hotel chain acquired the building, converting it into an hotel and suite of serviced apartments.

Address: No. 10 Trinity Square, EC3N 4AJ
Built: 1913–22
Listed Status: Grade II*
Public Access: Yes
Tube: Tower Hill
Website: fourseasons.com/tentrinity

49. Trinity House

Trinity House is the HQ of an organisation of the same name. Established by Henry VIII in 1514 to administer Britain's coastline and the lighthouses that protect it, its role, now also encompassing buoys and lightships, is revealed through external decorative reliefs with plump putti holding ropes and maritime instruments, flanked by lighthouses. Four cannons marked with sword-wielding lions guard the building, which is topped with a weathervane in the form of a gilded ship.

First situated at Deptford, the organisation relocated to Shadwell in 1618 and then to Stepney in 1660, when an additional building was acquired in the City but was destroyed during the 1666 Great Fire. The rebuilt City HQ was later consumed by fire, and between 1794 and 1796 Samuel Wyatt designed this classical building, with Trinity Square Gardens laid out shortly afterwards. Following the Blitz only the front façade survived, but thanks to photographic documentation it was largely reconstructed and the weathervane installed. A wing in contrasting brick was added but set back to retain the 1790s frontage. It contains the library, reading room, offices and the Pepys Room, named after the seventeenth-century diarist and Navy official who lived close by in Seething Lane.

A 1990s refurbishment restored much of the original 1790s interior decoration and inside, moving from one wing to another the difference between old and new is barely discernible.

Today Trinity House maintains sixty-six lighthouses and 450 buoys and inspects oil and gas rigs and wind farms. Their charitable arm is recalled in Mile End, where Trinity Hospital almshouses (now Trinity Green and in private ownership) date from 1695. At Bow Creek, Trinity Buoy Wharf comprises an artists' enclave and residential blocks, built within the Trinity House complex originally used for maritime lighting experiments. Michael Faraday was its Scientific Officer between 1836 and 1865 (see Entries 6, 25).

Address: Tower Hill, EC3N 4DH
Built: 1794–98; 1950s
Listed Status: Grade I
Public Access: By appointment
Tube: Tower Hill
Website: www.trinityhouse.co.uk

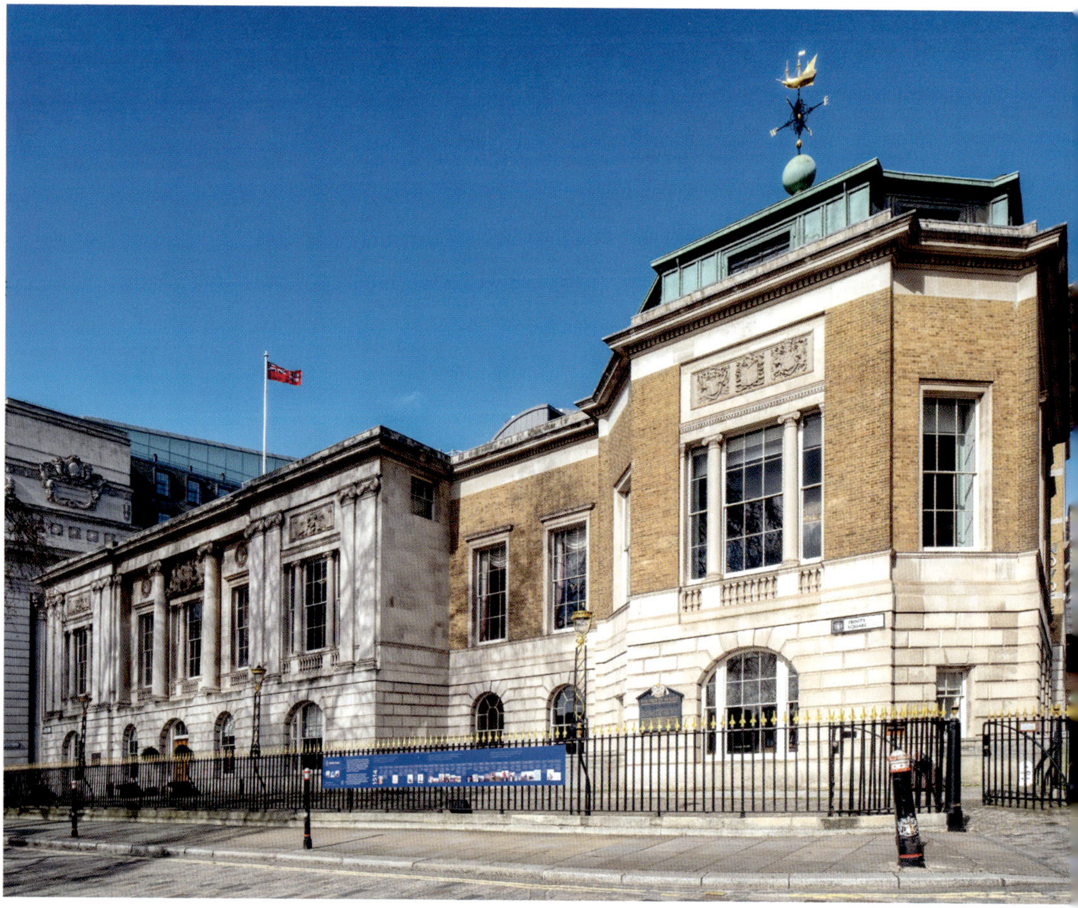

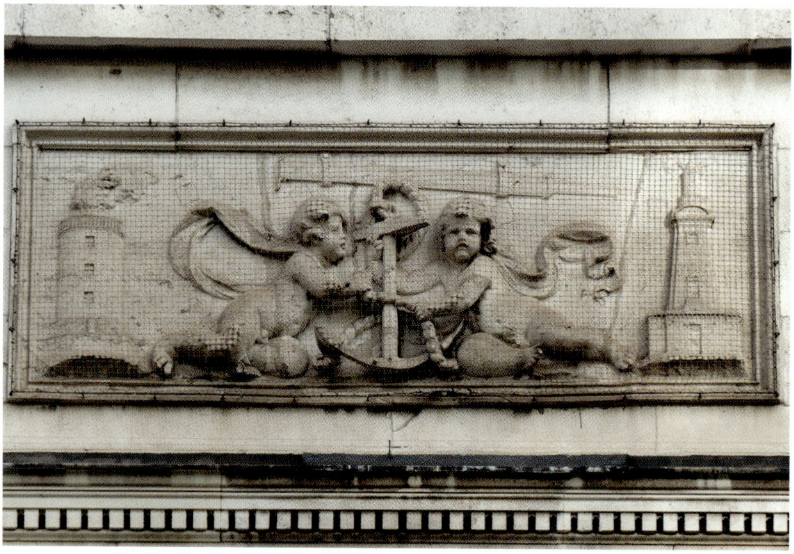

Above: Trinity House.

Left: Frieze with lighthouses, cherubs and anchor.

50. Tower of London

In its time His Majesty's Royal Palace and Fortress of the Tower of London has been a royal residence, stronghold, observatory, menagerie, mint, armoury and prison.

Construction commenced in 1078 by William I following his invasion of Britain in 1066 to subdue the 'vast and fierce populace' of London while at the same time protecting them. Its strategic riverside location prevented riverside attack.

From the pedestrianised piazza, the oldest section, the White Tower, is identifiable by four turrets and was the tallest structure in London when built. Inner and lower outer walls were built between 1190 and 1285, with more towers gradually added, now numbering over twenty. In front of the White Tower are the Devereux, Beauchamp and Bell towers, all once used to hold important prisoners.

A moat nearly 50 metres wide provided further defence. Drained in 1843 and used as allotments during the Second World War, it is now the 'back garden' for the 100 or so residents living on the premises, notably the governor and the Yeoman Warders, known as Beefeaters and easily recognisable in their Tudor-style uniforms. There are always at least six feathered residents, ravens, without which legend says London will fall.

Three lions in front of the moat, created out of galvanised wire by artist Kendra Haste, reference past diplomatic gifts of exotic animals to British monarchs which formed the nucleus of London Zoo when opened in 1828. Walking towards the river and onto

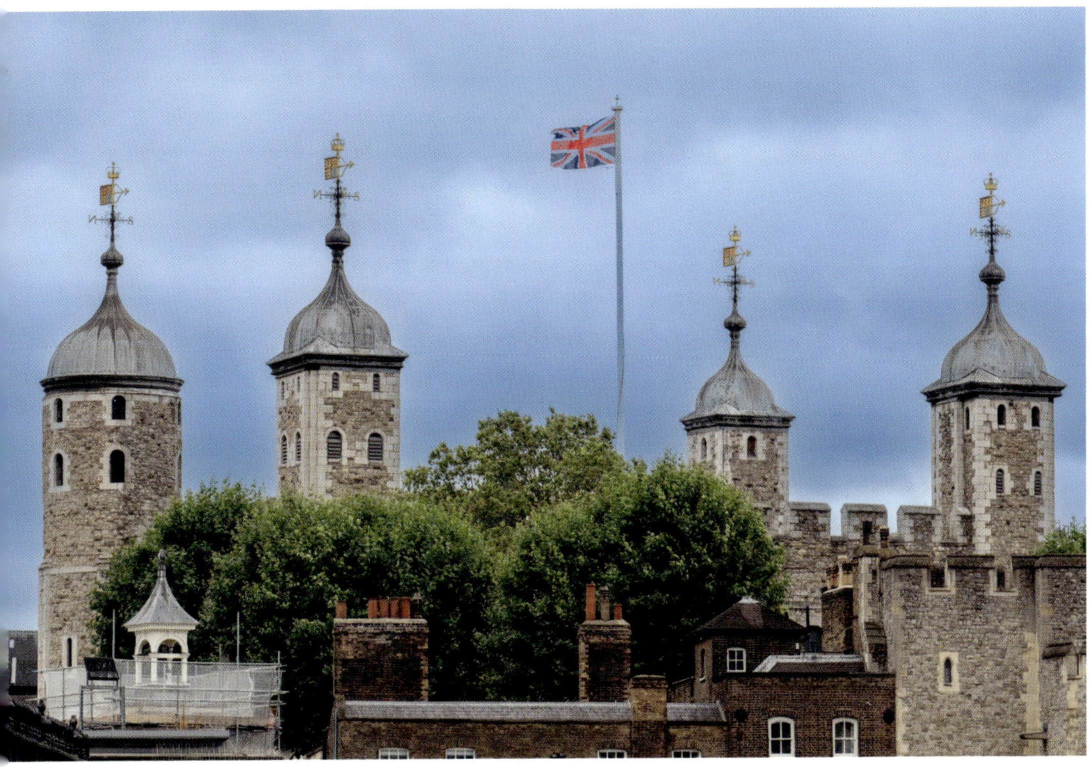

The White Tower, Tower of London.

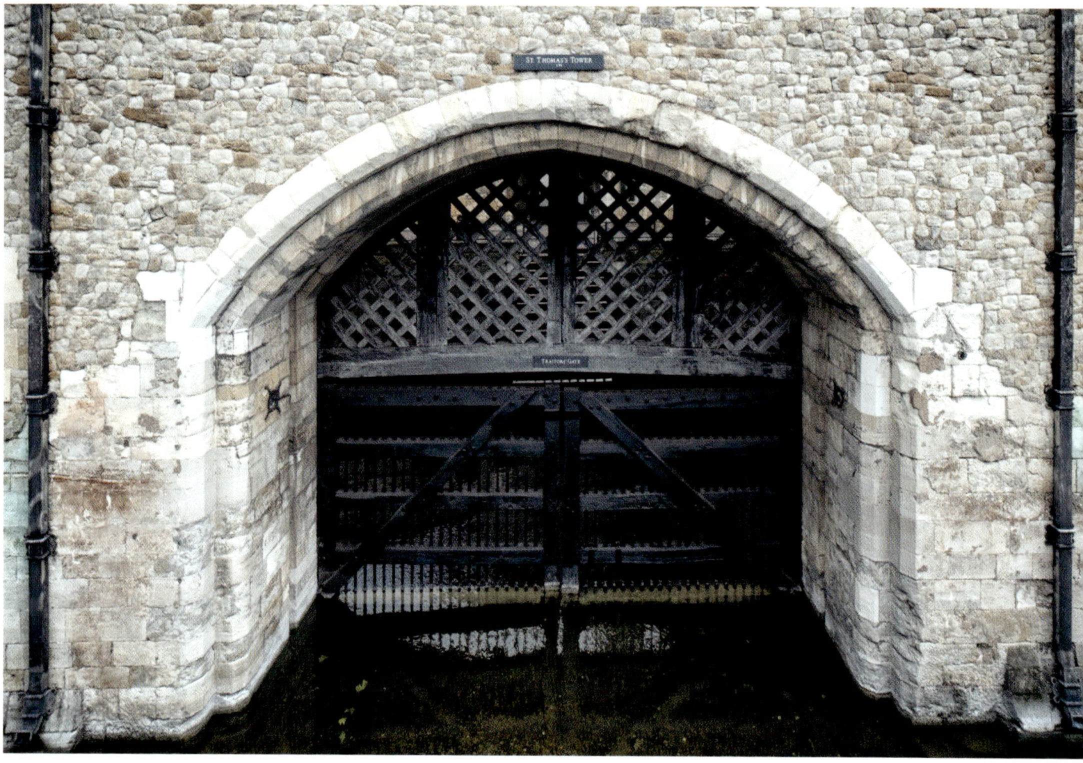

Traitors' Gate, Tower of London.

reclaimed land leads to Traitors' Gate, at the original water's edge and once the main exit and entry point for prisoners, as well as provisions and residents. Above is St Thomas's Tower, built in the 1270s and named in honour of St Thomas Beckett, who was murdered in 1170.

Eight prisoners, including three queens of England, were executed within the Tower precincts and 125 more on Tower Hill, now Trinity Square Gardens, the last taking place in 1747.

While there is much of the Tower to enjoy from the outside, those who enter can also explore the individual towers and view the priceless Crown Jewels.

Address: The Tower of London, EC3N 4AB
Built: 1076; various additions
Listed Status: Grade I (various); II (various)
Public Access: Yes
Tube: Tower Hill
Website: hrp.org.uk/tower-of-london

Acknowledgements

The authors would like to thank Amberley for commissioning this book and also acknowledge the following individuals for their assistance: City of London, Gardens Dept; Rachael Cannon, Hachette; Evelyn Watson, RSA; the King's Chapel of the Savoy; Gabriella Sotiriou, Two Temple Place; and Rosalind Zeffertt for her invaluable advice.

About the Authors

Louis Berk

Photographer and author Louis (louisberk.com) has collaborated with Rachel on four books, *Whitechapel in 50 Buildings*, *Secret Whitechapel*, *Whitechapel Doors* and *London's South Bank in 50 Buildings*. His photography regularly appears in newspapers, books, magazines and on the internet. When not working he is in the employ of his five cats or following his passion for wildlife photography, especially the local urban foxes.

Rachel Kolsky

Engaging, knowledgeable and entertaining, Rachel is a popular London Blue Badge Tourist Guide (golondontours.com) whose walks and talks focus on the 'human stories behind the buildings'. She has published six books, four with Louis, as well as *Jewish London* and *Women's London*, was a Trustee of her local independent cinema, The Phoenix, for over twenty years and has been a guest lecturer on cruises since 2009.

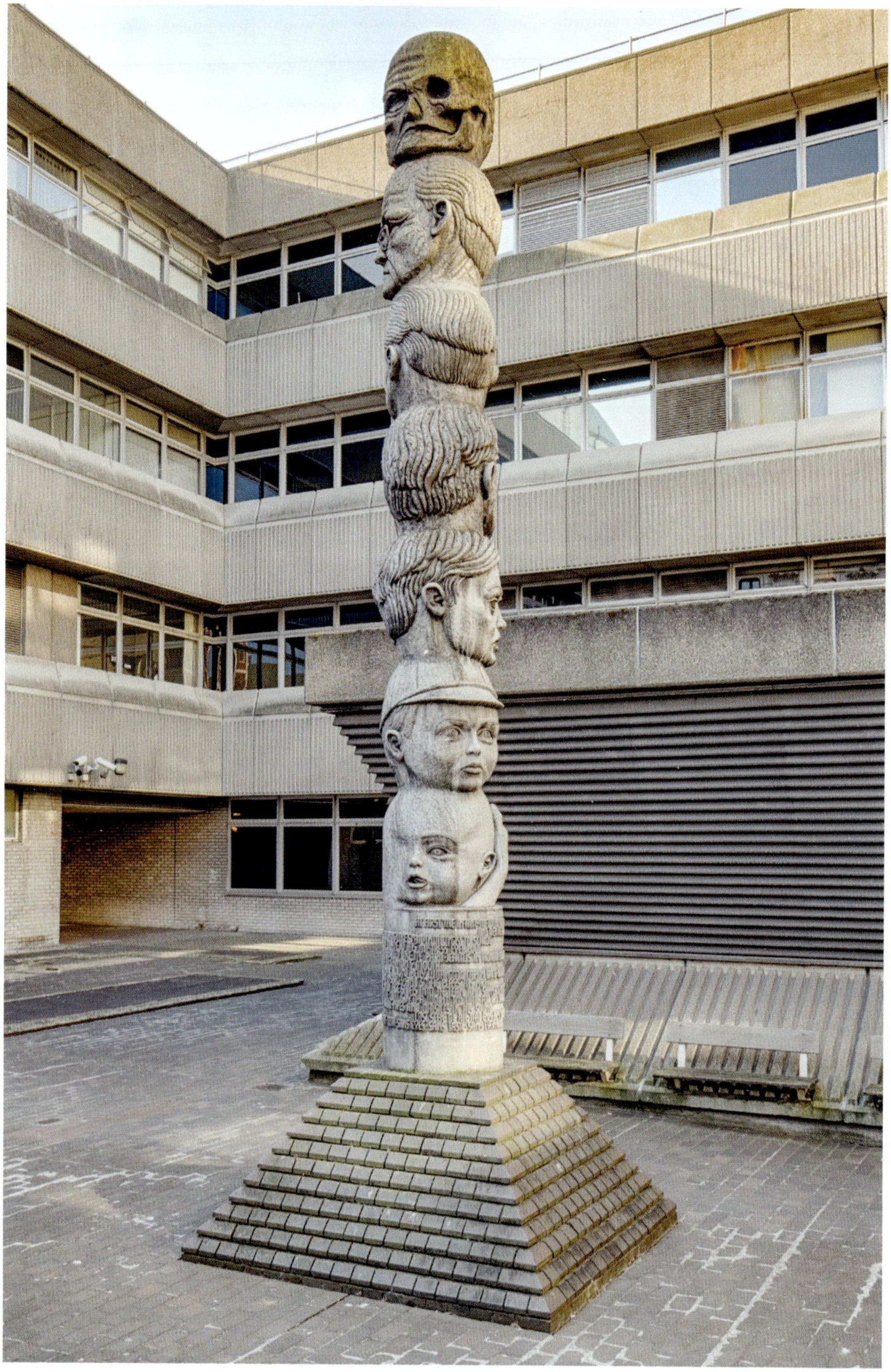

Seven Ages of Man by Richard Kindersley, Baynard House.